Business English Frameworks

Paul Emmerson

CAMBRIDGE
UNIVERSITY PRESS

PUBLISHED BY THE PRESS SYNDICATE OF THE UNIVERSITY OF CAMBRIDGE
The Pitt Building, Trumpington Street, Cambridge, United Kingdom

CAMBRIDGE UNIVERSITY PRESS
The Edinburgh Building, Cambridge CB2 2RU, UK
40 West 20th Street, New York, NY 10011–4211, USA
477 Williamstown Road, Port Melbourne, VIC 3207, Australia
Ruiz de Alarcón 13, 28014 Madrid, Spain
Dock House, The Waterfront, Cape Town 8001, South Africa

http://www.cambridge.org

First published 2002

Printed in the United Kingdom at the University Press, Cambridge

Typeface Utopia 9/12pt. *System* QuarkXpress® [GECKO]

A catalogue record for this book is available from the British Library

Library of Congress Cataloguing in Publication data

ISBN 0 521 00455 1

Designed and produced by Gecko Ltd, Bicester, Oxon

Project managed by Amanda Maris

Contents

Introduction

Frameworks

What is a framework?

A framework is a sheet with blank spaces for students to make notes as preparation for a personalized speaking activity. The spaces have headings, diagrams and prompts to provide a framework (structure) for the discussion. In this book the spaces for notes (section 2 of every framework) are preceded by some preparation of vocabulary and ideas (section 1).

Why use frameworks?

- Frameworks generate a lot of known and new language within a clearly defined context. This gives the teacher the opportunity to correct, improve or supply language in a feedback slot.
- In real life, business people would typically write notes as preparation for a discussion or meeting – ideas are expressed more clearly and more fluently after a little preparation.
- Frameworks allow a very high level of personalization and are therefore motivating and enjoyable.
- Frameworks offer great flexibility of classroom management.
- Frameworks give the teacher a lot of business information about the students.
- Frameworks involve minimal preparation.

When can frameworks be used?

- With students who want to talk about their own jobs, companies and professional lives (so most frameworks are not appropriate for pre-experience students in the tertiary sector).
- With all class sizes from groups to one-to-one.
- With all levels from Intermediate to Advanced.

Classroom management

Are the students interested in the topic?

Frameworks are highly student-centred – the language will come from them, not from a coursebook – so for the activity to be a success, students must want to talk about the topic. To help teachers select the frameworks to use, this book contains a photocopiable topics checklist, which gives the framework title (see page 7). Students can indicate the topics they are interested in, but note that it is not necessary for all students to be interested in the same frameworks.

Same framework or different frameworks?

Same framework
Every student can prepare the same framework, with the discussion being in pairs, threes, small groups or with the whole class. This will produce a focused discussion on a topic of common interest.

Different frameworks
Alternatively, different students can prepare different frameworks. If students then work in pairs, there will be an information exchange. Student A will use their completed framework to provide information, explain and clarify, while Student B listens and asks questions. Student B can be given a blank copy of the framework so that he/she sees the structure and can ask appropriate questions. The students then change roles. This is appropriate for groups where students have different interests and backgrounds.

Regrouping pairs
An extension of the previous activity is to regroup the students into new pairs and ask them to explain what their previous partner said. Let the students know you are going to do this at the beginning, as it is a motivating way of ensuring good listening and information checking, and produces a lively classroom atmosphere.

Brainstorming and vocabulary checking

Section 1 of every framework is an activity to prepare vocabulary and ideas for the note-writing in section 2. This is your chance to find out what the students already know and allow them to share this with other students in the group. Unless time is short, ask students to work in pairs or small groups (threes often works well) to think of additional ideas and vocabulary. Circulate and help with vocabulary, then write key words on the board. Remember to include collocations or put the word in a phrase or sentence to show how it is used. Also include word stress where appropriate.

Note-writing in class or for homework?

Completing the notes (section 2 of every framework) can be done in class or for homework. If done in class, the teacher can go round and help with language, and the discussion activity (section 3) will probably follow in the same lesson. If done out of class, the students have more time to think and prepare and will come to the next lesson ready to begin with the discussion activity. The second option is often very successful if students have time to do it.

Discussion in pairs or groups? Or mini-presentations?

Pairs
Discussion in pairs will mean plenty of free speaking practice for the students – and remember that the two students can have different frameworks (see above). Students sometimes feel that during pairwork no one is there to check their language, and so the presence of the teacher circulating and taking notes for later feedback is important. Try to get students to change partners frequently so that they get a variety of peer interactions.

Groups of three

Discussion in threes often works well as the students are under less pressure, have more time to reflect and formulate questions, and there is always another person to keep the conversation going. Again, it's important to circulate and monitor the students' language.

Whole class

Whole-class discussions are usually lively, with a free flow of ideas and information. They are often a favourite with students. Here the teacher is likely to be involved as well, often as a kind of discussion facilitator, and language can be corrected or supplied on the spot. Doing this without stopping the flow of the discussion is a skill that can make the difference between a successful and an unsuccessful activity. In general, it is better to write down points and return to them later, supplying a word or correcting a grammar form only when a student stops and asks for it.

Mini-presentations

Another variation is for students to give mini-presentations to the group. If students are using diagrams, they can draw them on the board or photocopy them onto transparencies and use an overhead projector. A good task for the listeners is simply to think of three questions to ask the presenter at the end. Alternatively, they can be given a language task such as 'write down all the words you hear that you would like to be able to use yourself'. Mini-presentations often work well with more experienced business people who can make connections with what the speaker is saying. They also work well if group members need real-life practice at presenting information to a group.

Repeating the discussion

The *Extension* section of the Teacher's notes for most frameworks suggests repeating the activity in a later lesson. This is a very powerful technique for increasing fluency and vocabulary acquisition. Check with the students first if they would like to have another chance to practise speaking about this topic. Point out that in their real jobs they have to talk about topics many times. Then, after a gap of a few days, repeat the activity as pairwork with a different partner. The discussion will nearly always follow a different course and the familiarity with the language and ideas will give a real boost to the students' fluency.

Feedback

Feedback slot

The Teacher's notes for each framework have a *Feedback slot* heading to flag this essential part of the lesson. As a rule of thumb, allow feedback time of at least half the speaking time. For example, in a 60-minute lesson where students have prepared their frameworks for homework and are working in pairs, all the Student As will speak about their frameworks and answer Student Bs' questions for about 15–20 minutes, followed by 10–15 minutes of feedback. Then the Student Bs will have their turn followed by feedback.

While the students are speaking, circulate unobtrusively, making notes (see *Using the feedback sheet* below) and speaking only if asked a direct question. Answer questions briefly and quietly and then withdraw eye contact and continue circulating. The students need to keep focused on the discussion and on their partner. If they feel the teacher is giving important information to other students which they are missing, the discussion will stop and may be difficult to restart.

Before the feedback slot allow the students to 'de-role' by relaxing and joking for a few moments in class. They will not be receptive for language work immediately following a lively discussion. Then write language points selected from your notes one by one on the board. Give students a chance to supply words or correct mistakes first. Keep the feedback slot fast-paced, covering perhaps 10–15 items over 20 minutes. Use the following guidelines for the choice of language to feed back on:

- variety – a good mixture of vocabulary the students needed, recurrent grammar mistakes, pronunciation difficulties, word order problems, collocation development etc.
- language that is relevant to the class – the need or error may arise from just one student's output, but choose it for feedback if it will help most of the other students as well.
- useful language – international business English is simple and direct. Avoid 'authentic' language that is low-frequency or that other non-native speakers in the real world will probably not understand.
- language at the right level for the group – this includes remedial presentations of structures that the students know but cannot yet produce accurately. Avoid having to present a grammar point for the first time without preparation.
- good language production as well as needs and mistakes – receiving positive feedback is highly motivating for individual students, and also encourages the rest of the group to produce the same item.

Finally, remember this rule for boardwork: always give language in context.

Using the feedback sheet

Business English Frameworks has a photocopiable feedback sheet (see page 9). Teachers can, of course, make language notes on any piece of paper for their own reference, and if feedback is done on the board to the whole group, then the feedback sheet will not be necessary. However, there are situations when teachers want to write individual feedback sheets for students:
- while listening to a one-to-one student.
- while listening to mini-presentations when the teacher has time to make notes for personalized feedback.

In these situations giving a feedback sheet to each student will give a professional touch to the lesson and make it easier for them to review their mistakes out of class. Write good examples of language use in the first column of the sheet, along with words of encouragement, extra tips, collocations, word building points etc. Write mistakes in the middle column – the actual words that you hear. Draw an arrow across to the third column where you write the correct version. You can do the corrections while listening and give the sheet to the student at the end of the lesson, or you can do them after class and give the sheet in the next lesson. Include comments, usage notes, diagrams, pictures to explain vocabulary etc. Alternatively, give the feedback sheet to the students with the arrows to show that a correction is necessary but with the third column left blank. Ask them to correct their own mistakes and check with you later.

With a one-to-one student you can use the sheets as the basis for a revision session. After several lessons ask the student to give you back all the sheets they have collected in their file, and then test them by saying the mistakes (the words they originally used) and eliciting a correct version. For vocabulary items that the student didn't know rather than got wrong, elicit the item with a definition, situation etc.

Four scenarios

Teacher A

Teacher A is working in-company with three students from the same department. Fifteen minutes before the end of a lesson she hands out the same framework to them all. They do section 1 together, and then the teacher asks them to do the note-writing (section 2) before the next lesson. In the next lesson one student has done nothing, one has made a few notes, and one has spent some time making good notes. The teacher asks the latter to begin. The discussion soon takes off, and the teacher takes a back seat, writing individual feedback sheets for each student. There is no board in the room, so in the feedback slot she looks at each sheet in turn and selects a few mistakes that are relevant to the other students. She offers the student who made the mistake the chance to self-correct, then she asks the others, and then she supplies the answer. She adds a few comments about usage and moves on. At one point, she chooses a grammar point for feedback and the students become confused, so she says she will cover it in the next lesson and moves on. At the end of the lesson, she gives the feedback sheets to the students.

Teacher B

Teacher B has an evening class. There are usually about ten students, young professionals from a variety of backgrounds, but attendance is intermittent. Their grammar knowledge is good, but they lack fluency and want a lot of speaking practice. Using the checklist on page 7 he gives them different frameworks, according to their interests, as a homework task. The students have to check the vocabulary (section 1) in a dictionary and make a few notes in the diagram/table (section 2). In the next lesson some students have done this, some haven't, and some are new. The teacher matches the students in pairs so that someone who has done the homework works with someone who hasn't – the former explains their framework and the latter asks questions (using the *Useful language* sheet on page 8 if appropriate). Two new students are put together as a pair and spend a few minutes preparing their frameworks in class before beginning a discussion. The class is too big for individual feedback sheets so the teacher makes notes on a piece of paper and does whole-class feedback on the board at the end. In a later lesson he regroups the pairs and asks students to explain their frameworks again. This time he concentrates mainly on good points in feedback and congratulates the students on their progress in fluency.

Teacher C

Teacher C is working with a student one-to-one at their office – the student is very busy, often cancels lessons, and never has time for homework. She gives the student a framework at the start of the lesson, based on the checklist the student has completed on page 7. They work through section 1 together. Then the teacher gives the student a few minutes to look through section 2 and organize his/her thoughts, but in the end the student chooses not to write anything. The teacher turns on a cassette recorder to start recording the student, using section 2 of the framework herself as a structure to ask questions. At the end of the discussion, the teacher rewinds the cassette and plays the recording, stopping at errors or breaks in fluency and giving the student the chance to self-correct. She writes down notes for each point on a feedback sheet as they occur. At the end of the lesson she gives the completed sheets to the student to put in his/her file. Several lessons later they repeat the discussion. The student performs very well without using his/her notes, speaking more accurately and fluently. The teacher comments on this as encouragement.

Teacher D

Teacher D is working on an intensive course with a small, mixed nationality group of middle and senior managers. He gives each student the same framework at the beginning of a lesson, and works through section 1 with the group. They brainstorm in small groups and then he writes new ideas and vocabulary on the board as class feedback. He then gives them ten minutes to complete the framework in class, and while they are doing this he plays some quiet music on a tape recorder and corrects their homework. The teacher chooses to ask the students to give mini-presentations to the group rather than work in pairs, just for variety. The first student receives many questions at the end of their presentation and the discussion moves off at an interesting tangent. The teacher keeps out of the discussion and writes individual feedback sheets for all the students (not just the presenter) as they are talking. Then a second student gives a mini-presentation. The teacher decides to have a feedback slot, so he selects a few items from each sheet and does some group feedback on the board. Then he gives the individual sheets to the students for them to put in their files. Other students save their mini-presentations for a later lesson.

Topics checklist

Put a double tick (✓✓) next to topics you want to discuss. Put a single tick (✓) next to topics you are quite interested in. If you are not interested, write nothing.

Management

1 Organization structure ☐
2 What do managers do? ☐
3 Use of resources ☐
4 Customer needs ☐
5 Improving customer relations ☐
6 Managing change ☐
7 Company strategy ☐
8 Small companies and start-ups ☐
9 Problems and solutions ☐
10 Personal management qualities ☐
11 The international manager ☐
12 Business ethics: a case study ☐

Sales and marketing

13 SWOT analysis ☐
14 Market research ☐
15 Product design/R&D ☐
16 Product description and features ☐
17 Marketing mix: one product ☐
18 Marketing strategy ☐
19 Constraints on marketing strategy ☐
20 Marketing budget ☐

Finance and accounting

21 Profit and loss account ☐
22 Balance sheet ☐
23 Managing cashflow ☐
24 Company analysis ☐
25 Investment advice ☐

Production and operations

26 Production process ☐
27 Operations growth ☐
28 Quality management ☐
29 Logistics and transport ☐

Human resources

30 Pay and promotion ☐
31 Motivation through job satisfaction ☐
32 Recruitment and selection ☐
33 Training and team-building ☐
34 Industrial relations ☐

International trade

35 Trade and government policy ☐
36 Exporting ☐
37 Importing ☐
38 Manufacturing location ☐

Economic and social context

39 Globalization ☐
40 Social responsibility ☐
41 The changing workforce ☐
42 The future of work ☐

Information technology

43 IT management ☐
44 E-commerce ☐
45 Using business software ☐

Cultural awareness

46 Cultural values at work ☐
47 Cultural values in society ☐
48 Working in another culture ☐

Recent business news

49 Discussing news items ☐
50 Using an authentic text ☐

Useful language

Leading the discussion

Introducing an idea

The main issue here is ...
In my company, the most important thing is ...

Developing an argument

Firstly, ... secondly, ...
Also, ... / In addition, ...
The thing is, ... / Actually, ...
Of course, ... / Obviously, ...
So, ... / Therefore, ...
As regards ... / As far as ... is concerned, ...
In general, ... although ...
It's true that ... but on the other hand ...
So basically, ... / To put it simply, ...

Confirming

That's right.
Exactly.

Checking other people understand

Do you follow?
Do you see what I mean?
Are you with me?

Rephrasing if people don't understand

Sorry, what I meant was ...
Let me put it another way.

Keeping control of the conversation

So you see ...
Anyway, ...
And as you probably know ...
Well, as I was saying, ...

Finishing what you want to say

Sorry, can I just finish?
I'll come to that in a moment.

Not answering

That's not really my area, I'm afraid.
Sorry, I don't have that information to hand.

Giving the conversation to another person

Is it the same in your company?
Do you find the same thing?

Participating in a discussion

Saying you don't understand

Sorry, I don't quite follow you.
Sorry, I'm not sure what you mean.

Clarifying: asking for repetition

Sorry, can you go back?
I'm sorry, I didn't catch that.
Sorry, could you explain that again, please?

Clarifying: asking for more information

Could you be a little more specific?
Can you give me an example?

Clarifying: using your own words to check

So, in other words, you think that ... Is that right?
Are you saying ...?

Showing interest

Really?
Right. Sure.
Mhm. Uh-huh. Yeah.
That's interesting.
Yes, of course.
Do you?
'echo' questions e.g. *five hundred? all over the world?*

Interrupting

Can I just ask something?
Sorry, could I stop you for a moment?
There's a question I'd like to ask.

Questions to continue the discussion

Could you say a bit more about ...?
I'd be interested to know ...
So what happens when ...?
So why do you ...?

Typical 'business' questions

So how is that financed?
How many people are involved?
What are the staffing/financial implications of that?
What are the implications for other departments?
How do you arrive at that figure?
What section of the market are you aiming at?
Does that involve much planning?
How does that compare with your competitors?
Is that a recent development?
What are your plans for the future?

Making notes

Can you give me a moment while I make a note?
How do you spell that?

 Paul Emmerson © Cambridge University Press 2002 **Photocopiable**

Feedback sheet

Name of student:			Date:
Good use of language	Mistakes	Corrections	

MANAGEMENT

1 Organization structure

Before you start

1 Are your students interested in this topic? Use the checklist on page 7.
2 Which classroom management options will you follow? See pages 4–5.
3 Do your students need language support for the discussions? See page 8.

1 Prepare.

1 Get students to discuss the words and phrases in pairs. Then check the meaning with the whole class. (See *Vocabulary box* below.)

Vocabulary box

sole trader: one person/family with their own business e.g. small shop, plumber, self-employed person. There is no distinction in law between them and the business, so they are personally liable for any debts.

partnership: two or more partners with a division of responsibilities and share of profits/risks e.g. management consultants, firm of accountants

private limited company: a small business or family company with directors. The company has *Ltd* after its name and it has a legal status independent of its owners, so they are not personally liable for any debts.

public limited company: a large company with shares quoted on the stock exchange. It has *PLC* after its name and it is 'public' because anyone can buy the shares.

multinational: a PLC that trades in several countries

state-owned enterprise: an organization that is still under government control, but might be privatized in the future

franchise: where a company gives a business the right to sell its goods in return for a share of the profit e.g. Body Shop, McDonalds, Benetton

2 Get students to add more examples to each list. Elicit examples and write them on the board. (See *Possible answers/ideas* box below.)

Possible answers/ideas

Department names: Finance/Accounts/Purchasing, Marketing/Sales/Customer Services, Production/ Maintenance/Distribution/Logistics, Human Resources/Personnel, Information Technology (IT)/Computer Services, Research and Development (R&D), Administration, Public Relations/Corporate Affairs, Legal

Other organization structures: by customer type, by work process (e.g. order fulfilment teams), by project team, by cross-functional teams (e.g. to solve a problem or work on a particular project)

3 Get students to brainstorm language to talk about their own job. Elicit examples and write them on the board. (See *Possible answers/ideas* box below.)

Possible answers/ideas

Phrases for talking about your job: I work in ..., My job title is ..., I deal with ..., I'm involved in ..., I'm in charge of ..., I have to handle ..., I report to ..., senior/middle/junior manager, line manager, flat/hierarchical structure, manufacturing/service sector

Job titles: The Board of Directors has a Chairman (UK)/President (US). The Board represents the interests of the shareholders. The company is

managed by the Managing Director (UK)/Chief Executive Officer (US). Other senior managers might include the General Manager (UK)/Chief Operating Officer (US), the Chief Technology Officer etc. The heads of the various departments are called Director (UK)/Vice President (US). Under the Directors is often a person with *Deputy* in their job title.

2 Draw a diagram and write notes.

1 Circulate while students draw their diagram. Write down on a piece of paper any useful language needed or produced. Write a few language items of general interest on the board at the end.
2 Get students to write notes on how their job relates to others. (See *Possible answers/ideas* boxes above for vocabulary.)

3 Give a mini-presentation. Ask for questions.

1 Explain that each student will give a mini-presentation to the class.
2 When it is their turn, let each student sit at the front and lead the session. Join the group as a participant, asking questions along with the other students e.g. *How is your organization structure changing?* Make a note of good/bad language use.

Feedback slot

See page 5.

1 Organization structure

1 Prepare.

1 Check the meaning of the following words and phrases.

sole trader, partnership, private limited company, public limited company, multinational, state-owned enterprise, franchise

2 Add more examples to each list.

Department names: <u>Finance, marketing,</u>

Other organization structures: <u>by product/service type, by geographical area,</u>

_____

3 Brainstorm vocabulary and phrases to talk about your job.

<u>I'm responsible for ...</u>

2 Draw a diagram and write notes.

1 Draw a diagram to show the structure of your organization or department.

2 Write notes on how your job relates to other jobs in the organization structure.

1 _____

_____

2 _____

_____

3 _____

_____

3 Give a mini-presentation. Ask for questions.

2 What do managers do?

1 Brainstorm.

1 Check comprehension of the examples. (See *Vocabulary box* opposite.) Then get students to brainstorm more phrases in pairs or small groups.

2 Elicit answers and write them on the board. (See *Possible answers/ideas* box below.)

Vocabulary box

forecast: to say what you expect to happen in the future; *forecast* is much more common in a business context than *predict*.
liaise: to speak to other people at work in order to exchange information with them

Tip

Point out the verb–noun collocations in the examples e.g. *motivate people*, and encourage students to produce more. For example, if a student says *I sell*, ask *What?* and *Who to?* and then write the collocations on the board.

Possible answers/ideas

As a manager, I ...
improve efficiency/productivity/company performance. analyse/solve/sort out problems, handle/investigate/look into/deal with/respond to complaints; set/fix/define goals/targets/objectives, decide/coordinate long-term strategy; communicate with/inform staff/employees, support/supervise/train staff, evaluate the performance of staff, give feedback to staff on their performance, set up/run appraisal systems; plan/set budgets, develop the

business, travel to other countries, recruit/dismiss/hire and fire staff, take/make/delegate decisions, keep records and files up-to-date; do market research, monitor competitors' activities, forecast costs, make investment decisions, deal with banks, prepare accounts; organize/take part in/chair meetings, write e-mails/letters, prepare reports, give presentations, negotiate with suppliers/customers/unions, meet with customers/the press/lobbies, set up/manage/ coach teams, set up/manage the website.

2 Complete the ideas map with your own management responsibilities.

1 Focus attention on the ideas map and check the vocabulary in the headings. Establish that students will write words/phrases/ideas at the end of each line, and that they can add more lines. They can also create new categories if necessary.

2 Circulate while students make notes. Write down on a piece of paper any useful language needed or produced. Write a few language items of general interest on the board at the end.

Tip

Keep a small set of ideas maps that students have completed in previous classes. Pass these round the group to show the general idea, but take them back before the students start their own maps. Alternatively, make a quick sketch on the board of your own responsibilities in the form of an ideas map – this also serves as a model.

Tip

Let students finish the ideas map in any way that makes sense to them – every student will complete it in a different way.

3 Discuss.

1 Which classroom management options will you follow? See pages 4–5.
2 Circulate during the discussion. Make a note of good/bad language use.

Tip

If students do mini-presentations to the whole class, photocopy the ideas maps and distribute one per student. This makes it easier for the others to follow and ask questions.

Feedback slot

See page 5.

Extension

- If you want a whole-class round-up, write on the board *one* of these topics for discussion: 'Management: an art or a science?', 'Three tips I would give to a new manager', 'The best/worst thing about being a manager is ...'
- Students can write a short summary of their own management responsibilities.
- Consider repeating the activity in a later lesson e.g. with a different partner. See page 5.

2 What do managers do?

1 Brainstorm.

As a manager, I ...

motivate people, control/forecast costs, take decisions, deal with suppliers,

give presentations, liaise with colleagues in other departments,

2 Complete the ideas map with your own management responsibilities.

3 Discuss.

3 Use of resources

Before you start

1 Are your students interested in this topic? Use the checklist on page 7.
2 Which classroom management options will you follow? See pages 4–5.
3 Do your students need language support for the discussions? See page 8.

1 Brainstorm.

1 Focus attention on the ideas maps and check the vocabulary in the headings. (See *Vocabulary box* below.)

Vocabulary box

know-how: a synonym for *knowledge*
skills: practical abilities that you can learn e.g.
  computing skills/language skills/communication
  skills/management skills

bank loan: an amount of money that you borrow and
  pay back over time
overdraft: the facility to have a temporary negative
  balance on your current account
premises: buildings that a company uses

2 Get students to brainstorm further vocabulary in pairs or small groups.
3 Elicit answers and write them on the board. (See *Possible answers/ideas* box below.)

Possible answers/ideas

Human resources: professionalism/motivation/creativity
etc. of staff, the variety and diversity of the workforce,
the entrepreneurial ability of senior managers
Financial resources: cashflow (cash available – not the
same as profits), IPO (initial public offering of shares,
when the company is floated on the Stock Exchange),
the further issuing of shares at a later date, venture
capital (for start-ups), instruments for risk management
like futures and options, derivatives, hedge funds

Material resources: land, raw materials, stock, vehicles
e.g. cars, vans, trucks
Technology: company information systems e.g.
accounting software, payroll software, customer
relations management software; new production
methods, storage systems in warehouses, use of intranet
e.g. staff profiles, database of know-how etc., use of
extranet e.g. product information, order tracking etc.

2 How can you use your resources more efficiently and more effectively? Write notes.

1 Check comprehension of the instructions to the
task – *efficiently* = 'without waste' and *effectively*
= 'producing the result that you want'.
2 Focus attention on the diagram and check the
vocabulary in the headings. Point out that there
is an extra box headed *Time* which doesn't appear
in section 1. Explain that this gives students a
chance to talk about time management.
3 Circulate while students make notes. Write
down on a piece of paper any useful language
needed or produced. Write a few language items
of general interest on the board at the end.

Tips

• For lower-level students paraphrase the instructions
as 'how can you use your resources better?'
• The phrase *your resources* in the instructions is
deliberately vague to allow students to write notes on
whatever interests them. If students need prompting, ask
them to focus on either the resources that they themselves
control, or those of their department/business unit.

Tip

Remind students to make a few notes in the *Customer
feedback* area of the framework i.e. how customer
feedback can make use of resources more effective.

3 Discuss.

1 Which classroom management options will you follow? See pages 4–5.
2 Circulate during the discussion. Make a note of good/bad language use.

Feedback slot

See page 5.

Extension

• Ask students why certain resources are not being used as efficiently/effectively as possible.
• Students can write a short summary of their own use of resources, or that of their partner.
• Consider repeating the activity in a later lesson e.g. with a different partner. See page 5.

3 Use of resources

1 Brainstorm.

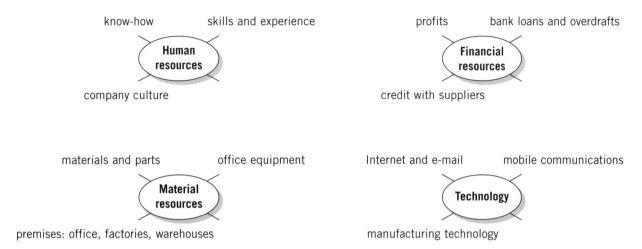

know-how   skills and experience

Human resources

company culture

profits   bank loans and overdrafts

Financial resources

credit with suppliers

materials and parts   office equipment

Material resources

premises: office, factories, warehouses

Internet and e-mail   mobile communications

Technology

manufacturing technology

2 How can you use your resources more efficiently and more effectively? Write notes.

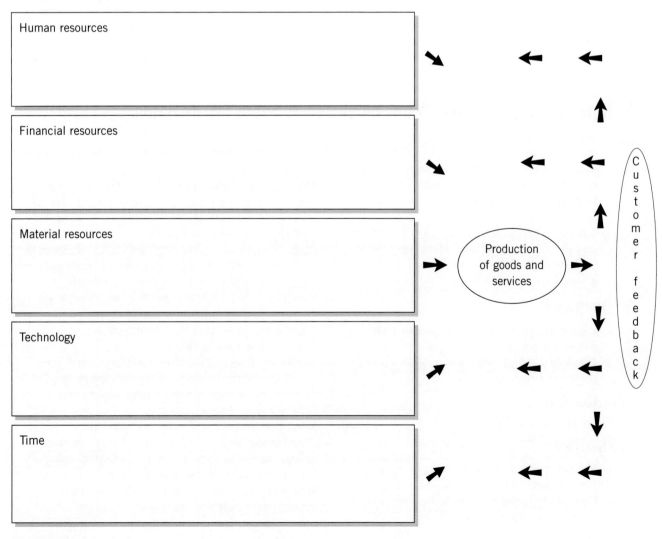

Human resources

Financial resources

Material resources

Technology

Time

Production of goods and services

Customer feedback

3 Discuss.

4 Customer needs

1 Brainstorm.

Tasks 1 and 2

1 Get students to brainstorm vocabulary for tasks 1 and 2 in pairs or small groups.
2 Elicit answers and write them on the board. (See *Possible answers/ideas* box below.)

Tip

Point out that, in general, the word *customer* is more common in the manufacturing sector and where cash is exchanged e.g. in shops and restaurants, while *client* is more common in the service sector.

Possible answers/ideas

1 **Before purchase:** continuity of supply, credit schemes, availability, price stability
   At the point of sale: warranty information, merchandising, resale future value
   After purchase: availability of spares, fault-free product life
2 **Manufacturer:** continuity of supply, advance notice of price increases for parts and raw materials, meeting quality standards
   Wholesaler: ongoing product quality, special packs with large quantities of goods, strong yet easy-to-move packing materials

Retailer: attractive packaging, point-of-sale merchandising, pricing policy that allows a reasonable profit, a fast and efficient ordering/delivery system, no faulty products, top-quality warranties
Service sector customer: good brochures and leaflets to support the sale of the service, top-quality warranties that are easy to understand
Consumer/End user: good design and build, easy-to-understand product/service information, availability, high levels of warranty protection, good after-sales service, occasional after-sales contact to show long-term commitment to the relationship

2 How does your company focus on customer needs? Write notes.

1 Focus attention on the diagram and check the vocabulary in the headings. Point out that the diagram shows the different stages of business activity, starting with R&D (Research and Development). Tell students that they don't have to fill in every section.
2 Circulate while students make notes. Write down on a piece of paper any useful language needed or produced. Write a few language items of general interest on the board at the end.

3 Discuss.

1 Which classroom management options will you follow? See pages 4–5.
2 Circulate during the discussion. Make a note of good/bad language use.

Feedback slot

See page 5.

Extension

- Students can write a short summary of the needs of their own customers.
- Consider repeating the activity in a later lesson e.g. with a different partner. See page 5.

Tip

Use the following prompts if the students have problems getting started:
R&D (Research and Development): How does feedback from the end user come back to the R&D department? How are design, specification and user-friendliness influenced by customer needs?
Production: How are quality, range and choice influenced by customer needs? How does information on recalls and repairs come back to the production department?
Marketing: How do customer needs influence price and product information? How is market research done? How is packaging designed? What types of merchandising are there?
Distribution: How do the distribution channel and sales locations depend on customer needs? How is speed of delivery maximized? Is there a sales tracking system and how does it help customers?
Sales: How do sales staff make available to other departments their first-hand knowledge of customer needs, how customers use the product, what customers see as the strengths and weaknesses etc.?
After-sales: How are complaints handled? Are there surveys and questionnaires of existing customers? How is knowledge of after-sales staff made available to other departments?

4 Customer needs

1 Brainstorm.

1 What do customers want? Add examples to the following lists.

Before purchase: _design, information,_

At the point of sale: _choice, demonstrations,_

After purchase: _good handling of complaints, maintenance/servicing,_

2 Add some special needs for each of the following types of customer.

Manufacturer: _keeping delivery schedules,_

Wholesaler: _capacity to deal with fluctuating orders,_

Retailer: _national advertising of brands,_

Service sector customer: _top-quality information about benefits to the final customer,_

Consumer/End user: _a long, trouble-free operational life of goods and services,_

2 How does your company focus on customer needs? Write notes.

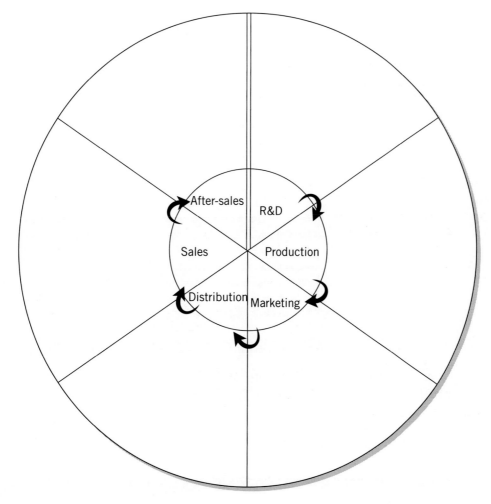

3 Discuss.

5 Improving customer relations

Before you start

1 Are your students interested in this topic? Use the checklist on page 7.
2 Which classroom management options will you follow? See pages 4–5.
3 Do your students need language support for the discussions? See page 8.

1 Prepare.

Tasks 1, 2 and 3

1 Divide the students into small groups and get them to answer the questions.
2 Elicit answers from the groups. (See *Possible answers/ideas* box below.)

Tip

In number 3, **a** is a general question with possible answers in the box below. Questions **b** and **c** are potentially controversial and so are best dealt with lightly and quickly, especially in an in-company group.

Possible answers/ideas

3a Customer satisfaction can be measured by: the number of complaints, number of compliments, number of customers repurchasing the same product, number of returned products, number of warranty claims, number of sales coming from recommendations of existing customers, how successful you are at cross-selling other products, figures for the duration of the business relationship, figures for the frequency of orders, number of lost customers and analysis of why you lose business.

3c Customers complain about: late delivery, wrong goods delivered, wrong number of goods delivered, right model but wrong colour, goods faulty/broken/damaged on unpacking, goods don't match specifications/expectations, wrong information on paperwork (delivery note/invoice/credit note/statement), omission of documentation such as warranty card/manual, misleading promotional material, unavailable product information, rude and unhelpful sales staff.

2 How are you improving customer relations? Write notes.

1 Focus attention on the grids and check the vocabulary in the headings. (See *Vocabulary box* below.)

Vocabulary box

printed material: this includes brochures, catalogues, leaflets etc.
reliability (n)/reliable (adj): a reliable product is one that you can depend on.
environmental profile: this includes use of recycled materials, biodegradability, production of waste products during manufacture etc.

2 Circulate while students make notes. Write down on a piece of paper any useful language needed or produced. Write a few language items of general interest on the board at the end.

Tip

If students can't get started because they feel that customer relations are already good, ask them to write about improvements they made in the past. Other prompts that may be useful include:
General issues: your image in the press and media? staff independence to make decisions?
Customer service issues: staff training? flexibility of staff? response times? your customers' ease of access to relevant staff? warranty (guarantee) arrangements?

3 Discuss.

1 Which classroom management options will you follow? See pages 4–5.
2 Circulate during the discussion. Make a note of good/bad language use.

Feedback slot

See page 5.

Extension

- Write the following titles on the board and ask students to tell a personalized story about one of them: 'How I turned a complaint into an opportunity', 'The angriest customer I ever had and how I dealt with him/her', 'The internal market in my company: now my colleagues are my customers'.
- Students can write a short summary of how to improve customer relations in their company.
- Consider repeating the activity in a later lesson e.g. with a different partner. See page 5.

5 Improving customer relations

1 Prepare.

1 Tell other students about an experience you had of excellent customer service.

2 Tell other students about an experience you had of very bad customer service.

3 a How can customer satisfaction be measured?

  b How does your company measure customer satisfaction?

  c What do your customers complain about? Why do you lose business?

2 How are you improving customer relations? Write notes.

General issues	
Company image	Company culture, including top-management leadership and middle-management support

Customer service issues			
Behaviour and product knowledge of sales staff	Printed material (catalogues etc.)	After-sales support	Handling complaints

Product issues			
Quality and reliability	Design and appearance	Distribution and delivery	Environmental profile

Using customer relations to develop the business	
Using customer relations to identify new products and markets	Using customer relations to identify opportunities for better financial performance

3 Discuss.

MANAGEMENT

6 Managing change

1 Prepare.

Task 1

Give students time to think of examples from their own company. Then get individual students to tell the rest of the class.

Tip

It isn't necessary for every student to cover every point. Ask students to think of just one or two examples each from the list and then tell the class.

Task 2

1 Check students understand that the vocabulary items are all collocations related to managing change. Get students to fill in the missing vowels. Then check the answers. (See *Answers* box below.)

Answers

1 to *cause / identify / acknowledge / face / be faced with / deal with / overcome* a problem
2 to *draw up / introduce / roll out / monitor / carry out / consolidate* a change programme

3 to *allocate / delegate / carry out / perform / complete* a task
4 to complete the change *on time / late / within budget / over budget*

2 Check comprehension of the vocabulary items. (See *Vocabulary box* below.)

Vocabulary box

to acknowledge: to accept that something is true
to face: to have to accept and deal with
to overcome: to succeed in dealing with or controlling a problem; to solve a problem
to draw up: to think of and plan
to roll out: to introduce a new system (or to launch a new product)
to monitor: to check the progress of
to carry out: to do something that needs to be organized and planned
to allocate: to give something officially for a particular purpose
task: a piece of work, a job

Tip

For higher-level groups, write up the words *a reactive/proactive response to a situation* and elicit the meaning: *a reactive response* is when change is forced on you because a problem happens; *a proactive response* is when you prepare for change because you see a problem before it happens.

2 Write notes about a major change that you helped (or will help) to manage.

1 Focus attention on the grids and check the vocabulary in the headings.
2 Circulate while students make notes. Write down on a piece of paper any useful language needed or produced. Write a few language items of general interest on the board at the end.

Tip

The following are possible ideas for why change is/was necessary in the *Background* box:
restructuring: changing the way that a company is organized or financed
downsizing: a reduction in the number of employees
a merger: when two companies join together to make one
an acquisition: when one company takes over another i.e. buys a majority or all of the shares of another

3 Discuss.

1 Which classroom management options will you follow? See pages 4–5.
2 Circulate during the discussion. Make a note of good/bad language use.

Feedback slot

See page 5.

Extension

- Students can write a short summary of the process of managing change.
- Consider repeating the activity in a later lesson e.g. with a different partner. See page 5.

6 Managing change

1 Prepare.

1 Give examples from your company of when the following things needed to change:
- tasks, job designs, business objectives
- attitudes and skills of employees
- the company culture
- operations technology and information technology
- the structure of the organization, including lines of authority and communication

2 Fill in the missing vowels in these words and check the meaning.

1 to c_ _s_ / _d_nt_fy / _ckn_wl_dg_ / f_c_ / b_   f_c_d w_th / d_ _l w_th / _v_rc_m_   a problem

2 to dr_w   _p / _ntr_d_c_ / r_ll   _ _t / m_n_t_r / c_rry   _ _t / c_ns_l_d_t_   a change programme

3 to _ll_c_t_ / d_l_g_t_ / c_rry   _ _t / p_rf_rm / c_mpl_t_   a task

4 to complete the change   _n t_m_ / l_t_ / w_th_n b_dg_t / _v_r b_dg_t

2 Write notes about a major change that you helped (or will help) to manage.

Background		
What is/was the change?	Why is/was it necessary?	How did you know?

	Action Plan/Tasks	Results
Design: agreeing on the vision, building the team, obtaining consensus		
Planning: developing the plan, allocating resources, agreeing on the timescale		
Implementation: roll out of change, communicating with stakeholders, overcoming resistance		
Consolidation: monitoring progress, minimizing negative effects, providing support		

Evaluation

3 Discuss.

7 Company strategy

1 Prepare.

1 Get students to check the meaning of the phrases in pairs. Then check with the whole class. (See *Vocabulary box* below.)

Vocabulary box

merger: when two companies join together to make one
acquisition: when one company takes over another
joint venture: a business activity in which two or more companies are working together on an individual project or in a particular market (one of them is often the local partner)

downsizing: a reduction in the number of employees
focusing on core activities: concentrating on the main, central activities that are most profitable

2 Get students to add examples of long-term strategies to the list.
3 Get students to brainstorm arguments for and against mergers. Elicit students' answers to tasks 2 and 3 and write them on the board. (See *Possible answers/ideas* box below.)

Possible answers/ideas

Other long-term strategies	Arguments for mergers	Arguments against mergers
licensing a trademark/patent (selling the right to manufacture something, usually in a foreign market), franchising (a company gives a business the right to use its name and sell its products in return for a fee or share of the profits), developing brands (products or company names that are easily and widely recognized), identifying market niches (gaps), selling assets (land, buildings etc.)	• increased market share • wider customer base (different market segments) • more purchasing power • economies of scale • better distribution channels • stronger management (additional know-how) • potential for benchmarking between the two companies (taking the best practice of each) • financial advantages on the balance sheet (ratio of debt to equity)	• rationalization may cause redundancies and closure of premises • management styles and company cultures may clash • cost of merger may cause cashflow problems • incompatibility of business/technical/IT systems • danger of losing some short-term momentum while management focuses on merger • larger company may be less flexible and responsive to change

2 Write notes.

1 Focus attention on the grids and check the vocabulary in the headings.
2 Circulate while students make notes. Write down on a piece of paper any useful language needed or produced. Write a few language items of general interest on the board at the end.

Tip

This framework helps students to talk about their own company strategy. However, it could be used to discuss the strategy of another company e.g. one in the news. In this case, you may want to make a copy of the framework with the *Implications for me and my area of work* heading blanked out.

3 Discuss.

1 Which classroom management options will you follow? See pages 4–5.
2 Circulate during the discussion. Make a note of good/bad language use.

Feedback slot

See page 5.

Extension

• Students can write a short summary of their company's strategy, or that of their partner.
• Consider repeating the activity in a later lesson e.g. with a different partner. See page 5.

7 Company strategy

1 Prepare.

1 Check the meaning of the following phrases.

internal growth (product development, market development, innovation); growth through mergers, acquisitions and joint ventures; defensive strategies (downsizing, restructuring, cutting costs, improving efficiency, selling parts of the business to focus on core activities)

2 What other long-term strategies can a company have? Add examples to the above list.

3 Brainstorm arguments for and against mergers.

2 Write notes.

What factors are influencing long-term strategy in your company?	
Macroeconomic trends and government policies	Market trends
Activity of competitors	Internal company factors (finance, R&D etc.)

Main elements of long-term strategy	Implications for me and my area of work
1	⇨
2	⇨
3	⇨

Possible problems with the strategy	Possible solutions
1	⇨
2	⇨
3	⇨

3 Discuss.

MANAGEMENT

8 Small companies and start-ups

Before you start

1 Are your students interested in this topic? Use the checklist on page 7.
2 Which classroom management options will you follow? See pages 4–5.
3 Do your students need language support for the discussions? See page 8.

1 Prepare.

1 Get students to read the text and check the vocabulary. (See *Vocabulary box* below.)

Vocabulary box

SME: small or medium enterprise. (This is quite a well-known term, and other countries often have an acronym for the same idea.)

start-up company: used to describe a new company

Tip

The text assumes that entrepreneurs only work for small and medium-size companies, which is usually true. Entrepreneurs hate routine and if their company gets too big, they often sell it and start again, or hand over control to someone else. However, some large organizations feel there is a place for entrepreneurial ideas, and a discussion point could be 'Can entrepreneurs work inside large organizations?'

2 Get students to describe an entrepreneur from their country.
3 Get students to discuss the question in pairs or small groups. (See *Possible answers/ideas* box below for possible input to the discussion.)

Possible answers/ideas

What are the special problems facing small companies?

Finance

Raising funds is a problem for small companies. The main sources are bank loans and overdrafts, loans from friends and relatives, capital introduced by the entrepreneur him/herself and venture capital.

Location

Size and location of the business premises are key issues for small companies. Good locations are expensive and hard to find.

Building a customer base

Small companies have a small number of customers. This allows them to focus and offer a more personalized service, but is also risky.

Exposure to risk due to limited product range

The company may grow quickly at the beginning because of an innovative product, but after some time larger companies will copy the product.

Cashflow

Most small business failure is due to poor cashflow management rather than a poor business idea. Firms can have a lot of orders but still go bankrupt because they don't have the cash (working capital) to pay bills.

Lack of specialist know-how

Founder members of the company often have more enthusiasm than experience, and small companies may have to bring in outside consultants as their business activities become more complex.

2 Do you work in a small or start-up company? Write notes.

1 Focus attention on the grids and check the vocabulary in the headings. (See *Vocabulary box* opposite.)
2 Circulate while students make notes. Write down on a piece of paper any useful language needed or produced. Write a few language items of general interest on the board at the end.

Vocabulary box

turnover: income/revenue

SWOT analysis: Strengths (company, positive points), Weaknesses (company, negative points), Opportunities (market, future chances), Threats (market, future dangers). See the Teacher's notes for framework 13 for examples of the four categories.

3 Discuss.

- Which classroom management options will you follow? See pages 4–5.
- Circulate during the discussion. Make a note of good/bad language use.

Feedback slot

See page 5.

Extension

- Students can give mini-presentations on the kind of business they would like to set up.
- Students can write a short summary of the issues discussed in the SWOT analysis.
- Consider repeating the activity in a later lesson e.g. with a different partner. See page 5.

8 Small companies and start-ups

1 Prepare.

1 Read the text and check the vocabulary.

Small and medium enterprises (SMEs) are started by entrepreneurs. Entrepreneurs are risk-takers who build new businesses around good ideas. They are innovative and creative and look for opportunities where others see only problems and threats. Entrepreneurs like independence and being in control. They have high energy levels and a strong motivation to succeed. They are action-oriented, they want to get things done quickly and they are happy to make difficult decisions. In the United States there are three million people starting new companies at any one time, and far more new jobs are created in SMEs than from the expansion of existing companies. Most small businesses fail in their first five years of operation, but that doesn't worry the entrepreneur. He or she just takes a break, learns the lessons and starts again.

2 Describe a well-known entrepreneur from your country.

3 What are the special problems facing small companies?

2 Do you work in a small or start-up company? Write notes.

Background
Size? Main products/services? Main customers? Main competitors?
Company history

Marketing strategy	Financial issues
Key features of existing products/services	Turnover and profits
Advertising and promotion	Cashflow and sources of finance
Pricing policy	
Distribution channels	**Human Resources issues**
New products/services	

SWOT analysis	
Strengths	Weaknesses
Opportunities	Threats

3 Discuss.

MANAGEMENT

9 Problems and solutions

Before you start
1 Are your students interested in this topic? Use the checklist on page 7.
2 Which classroom management options will you follow? See pages 4–5.
3 Do your students need language support for the discussions? See page 8.

1 Brainstorm.

Task 1

Get students to brainstorm problems they have at work and complete the ideas maps. Elicit a few examples. (There are no suggested answers here as these will vary from group to group.)

Task 2

1 Get students to add to the lists of verbs that collocate with *a problem* and *a solution*. Then check their answers. (See *Possible answers* box below.)

Possible answers

1 Other verbs that collocate with *a problem*: to approach, to cause, to define, to examine, to experience, to identify, to overcome, to present, to recognize, to resolve, to solve, to sort out, to tackle (to make an effort to deal with it – *tackle* is a term from football), to think over/through	**2 Other verbs that collocate with *a solution*:** to accept, to agree on, to aim at, to arrive at, to come up with, to look for, to offer, to propose, to reach, to reject, to seek, to work out (to find a solution after thinking carefully about it)

2 Elicit additional language for problem-solving and making suggestions. (See *Possible answers* box below.)

Possible answers

a solution / a way forward / a course of action	to look at a problem in another way/from another angle
the pros and cons = the advantages and disadvantages	to balance one argument against another
to consider the strengths/weaknesses of different options/alternatives	the likely effects/consequences of doing something

2 Think of a problem you are currently having at work, and two possible solutions. Write notes.

1 Focus attention on the grids and check the vocabulary in the headings.
2 Circulate while students make notes. Write down on a piece of paper any useful language needed or produced. Write a few language items of general interest on the board at the end.

3 Give a mini-presentation.

Task 1

1 Explain that each student will give a mini-presentation to the class.
2 When it is their turn, let each student sit at the front and lead the session.

Task 2

Get the class to brainstorm other solutions and vote for the best one. Sit away from the students and take notes. Make a note of good/bad language use.

Feedback slot

See page 5.

Extension

Students can write a short summary of their own problem and possible solutions, perhaps as a formal report to their boss. Alternatively, they can write a summary of one of the other cases.

Tip

In lower-level groups elicit useful language and leave it on the board during the presentations e.g.
Making suggestions: *How about ... (+ -ing) / Why not ... / It's just an idea, but why don't you ... / I know, maybe you could ...*
Agreeing: *That sounds like a good idea. / That might be worth trying. / Yes, I think that would work really well.*
Disagreeing: *I'm not sure about that because ... / I'm afraid I don't like that idea.*

Tip

Use any interesting cases to make a 'case study' worksheet for other classes, changing the original company name and any personal details.

9 Problems and solutions

1 Brainstorm.

1 What problems do you have at work? Complete the ideas maps.

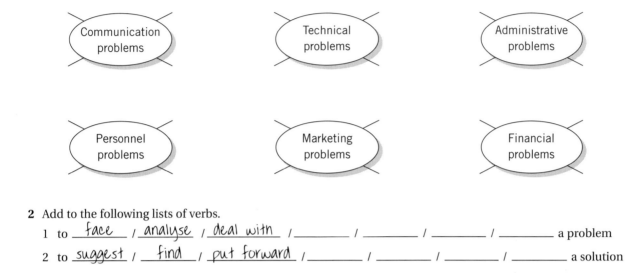

2 Add to the following lists of verbs.
1 to _face_ / _analyse_ / _deal with_ / _____ / _____ / _____ / _____ a problem
2 to _suggest_ / _find_ / _put forward_ / _____ / _____ / _____ / _____ a solution

2 Think of a problem you are currently having at work, and two possible solutions. Write notes.

Definition of the problem	Background and probable causes

Possible solution A

Strengths:	Weaknesses:
•	•
•	•

Possible solution B

Strengths:	Weaknesses:
•	•
•	•

3 Give a mini-presentation.

1 Present your problem and solutions to the group. Ask and answer questions.

2 Brainstorm other possible solutions. Which is the best solution?

MANAGEMENT

10 Personal management qualities

Tip

> Every business English student who is in work will find this framework
> relevant. Students with international experience at a higher level in their
> companies will find framework 11 offers them more opportunity to discuss
> their abilities in detail. See also the *Extension* section below for how to make
> this framework relevant to senior managers.

1 Prepare.

1 Get students to read through the management qualities 1–24 and check the vocabulary. (See *Vocabulary box* below.)

Vocabulary box

challenge: something new and different that needs a lot of skill and effort to do	*keeping up-to-date:* knowing the most recent information
setback: a problem that stops you from making progress	*being discreet:* being careful about what you say

2 Let students complete the *Job* and *Me* columns individually, following the instructions.

Tip

> You may want to point out that qualities 17 and 18 are to
> some extent opposites, as are 19 and 20. This should
> provoke more thought and discussion about these qualities.

2 Write notes.

1 Focus attention on the grids and check the vocabulary in the headings.
2 Circulate while students make notes. Write down on a piece of paper any useful language needed or produced. Write a few language items of general interest on the board at the end.

3 Discuss.

1 Which classroom management options will you follow? See pages 4–5.
2 Circulate during the discussion. Make a note of good/bad language use.

Feedback slot

See page 5.

Extension

- Students in more senior management positions may enjoy discussing 'Leadership', a topic not otherwise covered in these frameworks. As a warmer for this topic, write on the board 'How is leadership different from management?'. Continue the discussion. If you want more input for the discussion, here are six possible 'principles' of leadership:
  1 Challenge existing processes. Encourage innovation and support people who have ideas.
  2 Be enthusiastic. Inspire others through personal enthusiasm.
  3 Help others. Be a team player and support the efforts and abilities of other people.
  4 Set an example. Provide a role model for how others should act.
  5 Celebrate achievements. Bring emotion into the workplace and bring together hearts as well as minds.
  6 Vision. Have a clear sense of the future and communicate it to others.
- Students can write a short summary of their own personal management qualities, perhaps from the point of view of a Human Resources recruitment consultant writing a short report about them.

10 Personal management qualities

1 Prepare.

1 Study the management qualities below and check the vocabulary.

	Job Me
1 Having a good understanding of the market	☐☐
2 Having good product knowledge	☐☐
3 Having a good personal image (clothes, speech etc.)	☐☐
4 Being a good administrator and organizer	☐☐
5 Having the ability to motivate people	☐☐
6 Being good at organizing your time	☐☐
7 Knowing when to delegate and when to refer to a higher level	☐☐
8 Being flexible about plans and targets	☐☐
9 Liking challenges	☐☐
10 Being a good team member	☐☐
11 Being able to take risks	☐☐
12 Being able to recover quickly after a setback	☐☐

	Job Me
13 Having the ability to make difficult decisions under pressure	☐☐
14 Having good lines of communication with other staff	☐☐
15 Keeping up-to-date by training and reading	☐☐
16 Having a good understanding of other cultures	☐☐
17 Being strong and direct	☐☐
18 Being discreet and diplomatic	☐☐
19 Being sociable and cooperative	☐☐
20 Being independent and free-thinking	☐☐
21 Being honest and transparent	☐☐
22 Being a good talker	☐☐
23 Being a good listener	☐☐
24 Being able to go home and forget about work problems	☐☐

2 Look at the two columns.

- In the *Job* column put a tick (✓) for those qualities that you think are important in your job. Put a double tick (✓✓) for a few very important qualities.
- In the *Me* column put a tick (✓) for those qualities where you feel you are quite strong. Put a double tick (✓✓) for a few areas that are your real strong points. Put a question mark (?) for any areas where you feel you need further experience or training.

2 Write notes.

Choose two *Job* points with a double tick (✓✓). Why are they so important?

1

2

Choose two *Me* points with a double tick (✓✓). Give examples that demonstrate your abilities.

1

2

Choose two points where there is a difference between the *Job* and *Me* columns. Comment.

1

2

Other important qualities not included in the list

Job   Me

3 Discuss.

11 The international manager

Before you start

1 Are your students interested in this topic? Use the checklist on page 7.
2 Which classroom management options will you follow? See pages 4–5.
3 Do your students need language support for the discussions? See page 8.

Tip

This activity is really aimed at students who already consider themselves as international managers and who want a chance to talk about their skills and experience. It requires the students to be at a higher level of management (although not necessarily of language) than framework 10.

1 What skills does an international manager need? Brainstorm.

1 Focus attention on the ideas maps and check the vocabulary. (See *Vocabulary box* below.)

Vocabulary box

competitive advantage: something that helps a company to be more successful than its competitors
strategy: a general set of plans
objectives: specific targets/goals

uncertainty: not knowing what will happen
feedback mechanism: a process that makes it possible to know how good or useful something is (so that you can improve it)

2 Get students to brainstorm further vocabulary in pairs or small groups.
3 Elicit answers and write them on the board. (No suggestions are given here as the answers depend on individual situations and points of view.)

Tip

Point out that the final oval with the question mark is left for the students to think of their own ideas. If students can't think of anything for this final oval, some suggestions are: *Promoting knowledge across the organization, Turning threats into opportunities, Flexibility, Training self and coaching others* etc.

2 Write notes about your own experience and skills.

1 Focus attention on the grids and check the vocabulary in the headings. Remind students that the final box with the question mark corresponds to the oval with the question mark in section 1.
2 Circulate while students make notes. Write down on a piece of paper any useful language needed or produced. Write a few language items of general interest on the board at the end.

Tip

Tell students that they should make notes on specific activities/situations that they have actually done in their jobs. Point out that if they ever go for an interview for an international management position, they will have to give examples of their own experience in exactly this kind of way.

3 Discuss.

1 Which classroom management options will you follow? See pages 4–5.
2 Circulate during the discussion. Make a note of good/bad language use.

Feedback slot

See page 5.

Extension

- Students can write a short summary of their own management abilities, perhaps from the point of view of a Human Resources recruitment consultant writing a short report about them.
- Consider repeating the activity in a later lesson e.g. with a different partner. See page 5.

11 The international manager

1 What skills does an international manager need? Brainstorm.

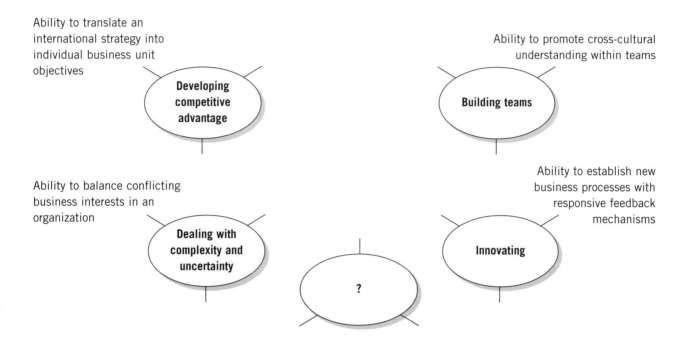

Ability to translate an international strategy into individual business unit objectives

Developing competitive advantage

Ability to promote cross-cultural understanding within teams

Building teams

Ability to balance conflicting business interests in an organization

Dealing with complexity and uncertainty

?

Ability to establish new business processes with responsive feedback mechanisms

Innovating

2 Write notes about your own experience and skills.

Developing competitive advantage

My experience

Building teams

My experience

Dealing with complexity and uncertainty

My experience

Innovating

My experience

?

My experience

3 Discuss.

12 Business ethics: a case study

Before you start

1 Are your students interested in this topic? Use the checklist on page 7.
2 Which classroom management options will you follow? See pages 4–5.
3 Do your students need language support for the discussions? See page 8.

1 Check the vocabulary and continue the lists.

Tasks 1 and 2

1 Get students to read through the lists in tasks 1 and 2 and check the vocabulary. (See *Vocabulary box* below.)

Vocabulary box

ethics: rules of behaviour used to decide what is right and wrong (*ethical behaviour ≠ unethical behaviour*)
bribery: giving money to someone dishonestly to persuade them to help you
kickback: (informal) money that a person gets for secretly and dishonestly helping someone
layoffs/redundancies: when workers' jobs are stopped because there is not enough work
diversity issues: these include race, gender, religion, sexual orientation

sexual harassment: threatening or offensive behaviour towards someone of the opposite sex
insider trading: when someone uses knowledge that is not available to other people in order to buy or sell shares
price fixing: when companies agree on the price they will charge in order to avoid competing with each other
whistleblower: someone who tells people in authority about dishonest or illegal practices
NGOs: non-governmental organizations e.g. Greenpeace, Save The Children, church organizations, single-issue pressure groups etc.

Tip

Teach higher-level students the word *stakeholder:* a person or organization that is involved in an issue, project, system etc., especially because they have a financial interest. Note that all the people listed in task 2 are stakeholders.

2 Get students to continue the lists.

Tip

The lists are quite comprehensive to help the students think of examples for the case study, so if they can't think of any more items, move on quickly.

2 Write notes.

Tasks 1 and 2

1 Establish that students will each introduce a case that they know about personally. It could be in their industry, a case they know about through a friend, or one that has been in the news recently.
2 Focus attention on the grids and check the vocabulary in the headings. (See *Vocabulary box* opposite.) Point out that in task 2 students don't have to fill in every box. Get students to write notes.
3 Circulate while students make notes. Write down on a piece of paper any useful language needed or produced. Write a few language items of general interest on the board at the end.

Vocabulary box

harm: damage, trouble caused
benefit: an advantage that you get from something
rights: things that you are allowed to do, legally or morally
responsibilities: things that you should do, legally or morally

Tip

Remind students to refer to the list in section 1, task 2 for possible people/things affected by the case.

3 Give a mini-presentation. Ask for questions.

1 Explain that each student will give a mini-presentation to the class.
2 When it is their turn, let each student sit at the front and lead the session. Consider joining the group as a participant asking questions yourself, or sit away from the group. Make a note of good/bad language use.

Tip

Use any interesting cases to make a 'case study' worksheet to use with other classes, changing the original company name and any personal details.

Feedback slot

See page 5.

Extension

Students can write a short summary of their own case study, perhaps as a formal report.
Alternatively, they can write a summary of one of the other cases.

12 Business ethics: a case study

1 Check the vocabulary and continue the lists.

1 What kind of business issues can have an ethical dimension?

dishonesty in communications with top management/clients/government agencies, dishonesty in advertising, low wages/poor conditions/child labour in factories overseas, doing business on the basis of friendship/family connections, problems with gifts/entertainment, bribery, kickbacks, government officials asking for 'consultancy fees', layoffs/redundancies, environmental issues, animal rights issues, employee privacy issues (e.g. data protection), diversity issues, sexual harassment, insider trading, price fixing, dumping

2 Who/What can be affected by unethical behaviour?

the whistleblower, key decision makers (individuals), co-workers, employees and their families, top managers/the board of directors, shareholders, customers, suppliers, competitors, government and its agencies, lawyers and courts, consumer groups, environmental groups, NGOs, other special interest groups, people in the local community, the environment (water, air, plants, animals, natural resources), future generations

2 Write notes.

1 Write notes about an ethical issue that you know about. You will present it to the group as a case study.

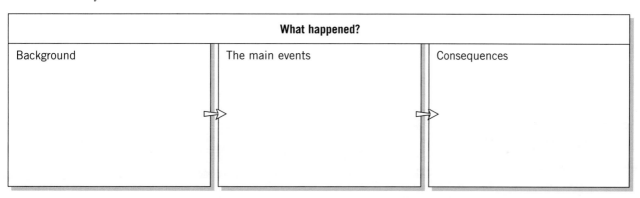

What happened?		
Background	The main events	Consequences

2 Choose five people/things affected by the case. Write notes in any relevant boxes.

	Harm	Benefit	Rights	Responsibilities
1 _____				
2 _____				
3 _____				
4 _____				
5 _____				

3 Give a mini-presentation. Ask for questions.

SALES AND MARKETING

13 SWOT analysis

Before you start

1 Are your students interested in this topic? Use the checklist on page 7.
2 Which classroom management options will you follow? See pages 4–5.
3 Do your students need language support for the discussions? See page 8.

1 Read the text and check the vocabulary.

Get students to read through the text and check the vocabulary. (See *Vocabulary box* below.)

Vocabulary box

Strengths

know-how: knowledge/expertise
brand: a product or company name that is easily and widely recognized
patent: a legal document giving a company the right to make or sell a new product and stating that no other company can do this

Weaknesses

industrial relations: the behaviour of workers and management towards each other (US = *labor relations*)
outdated: old-fashioned
lack of ...: not having ...
R&D: Research and Development

Opportunities

developments in technology: these could allow new production methods or new management information systems, as well as actually creating new products

Threats

market saturation: when there are too many products for sale
slowdown: when business activity is slower than before
recession: more serious than a *slowdown*, and is defined as two consecutive quarters of negative growth in the economy
regulation: an official rule or order, in this context probably new government legislation (laws)
shortage of ...: not having enough of ...

2 Write notes about your own company and market.

1 Get students to complete the grid.
2 Circulate while students make notes. Write down on a piece of paper any useful language needed or produced. Write a few language items of general interest on the board at the end.

3 Give a mini-presentation. Ask for questions.

1 Explain that each student will give a mini-presentation to the class.
2 When it is their turn, let each student sit at the front and lead the session. Consider joining the group as a participant asking questions yourself, or sit away from the group. Make a note of good/bad language use.

Feedback slot

See page 5.

Extension

Students can write a short report about their company, using the structure of a SWOT analysis.

Tips

- Point out the use of *poor* in the text rather than *bad*. Poor suggests 'not as good as it could be' and is better in a business context than the very strong and direct *bad*.
- As in all the frameworks (and in business usage), the word *products* does not just refer to manufactured products – it can also include financial products, services etc.
- Teach higher-level students the phrase *core competencies* – the special strengths that an organization has. They are things that give a competitive advantage and are difficult for competitors to duplicate e.g. special manufacturing technologies, special knowledge, unique product distribution systems etc.

Tip

Divide the board into four before students start their presentations. Students can write up points before/as they speak

13 SWOT analysis

1 Read the text and check the vocabulary.

A standard way to analyse the market position of a company is by a SWOT analysis. SWOT stands for Strengths, Weaknesses, Opportunities, Threats. The first two are internal, the second two are external.

▶ **Strengths** are strong points about the company. Examples include a good market share, strong financing with low levels of debt, know-how and experience of top management, a skilled and motivated workforce, an efficient manufacturing process, modern production technology, good production quality, a good reputation in the market (a good brand image), patents, well-established products, new products, good distribution etc.

▶ **Weaknesses** are weak points about the company. Examples include a small market share, high levels of debt, a weak management, poor management information systems, untrained and poorly motivated staff, poor industrial relations, outdated equipment or production methods, poor quality control, a lack of modern technology, past planning failures, a lack of R&D (and therefore innovation), a lack of new products, poor distribution etc.

▶ **Opportunities** are future chances. Examples include possible new markets, growth in the existing market, a strong national/global economy, competitors' mistakes, developments in technology etc.

▶ **Threats** are future dangers. Examples include market saturation, a slowdown (or recession) in the economy, rising interest rates, the success of existing competitors, new competitors, changing consumer tastes, substitute products, new regulations, political problems, a shortage of resources etc.

2 Write notes about your own company and market.

Strengths	Weaknesses
Opportunities	**Threats**

3 Give a mini-presentation. Ask for questions.

14 Market research

1 Prepare.

Task 1

Elicit answers to the questions as a whole-class discussion. (See *Possible answers/ideas* box below.)

Possible answers/ideas

What is market research?
- obtaining information about a market, including who is buying a product, how much they are buying, why they are buying it, and what else they might buy

Why do companies do it?
- to find information about consumer needs and preferences, consumer behaviour and buying patterns
- to find information about market trends, gaps in the market, the activity of competitors
- to test a range of possible advertising campaigns before a final decision is taken
- to focus efforts across the company
- to minimize risk and maximize returns generally

Task 2

Check comprehension of *sample* – a group of people who have been chosen to give opinions about something. Elicit answers to the question as a whole-class discussion. (See *Possible answers/ideas* box below.)

Possible answers/ideas

Issues in choosing the sample: size of sample; checking for factors such as age, sex, educational background, occupation etc.; proportion of users and non-users in the sample; generally making sure that the sample is 'statistically reliable' (i.e. it should give similar results to those produced if everyone in the target group was asked.)

Task 3

1 Check comprehension of the vocabulary in task 3. (See *Vocabulary box* below.)

Vocabulary box

desk research: collecting existing published information
field research: collecting new information by going out of the office and asking people directly
benchmarking: using one company's good performance as a standard by which to judge others
focus group: a group of consumers brought together to give opinions about products, adverts etc.

motivational/psychological research: collecting information about why people decide to buy one product or brand rather than another – this could be for reasons that the consumer him/herself is not aware of.
questionnaire: a written list of questions given to a large number of people to collect information

2 Get students to categorize the research methods and then check the answers. (See *Answers* box below.)

Answers

DR: analysis of sales figures, comparison with competitors, statistics, study of more developed markets
FR: face-to-face interviews, focus groups, motivational/psychological research, observation of consumer behaviour, questionnaires, telephone/street interviews, test marketing

2 Write notes about market research in your company.

1 Focus attention on the grids and ideas map and check the vocabulary in the headings.
2 Circulate while students make notes. Write down on a piece of paper any useful language needed or produced. Write a few language items of general interest on the board at the end.

3 Discuss.

1 Which classroom management options will you follow? See pages 4–5.
2 Circulate during the discussion. Make a note of good/bad language use.

Feedback slot

See page 5.

14 Market research

1 Prepare.

1 What is market research? Why do companies do it?

2 What issues are important in choosing the sample of people for the study?

3 Write DR (for desk research) or FR (for field research) by each of the following research methods:

- analysis of sales figures ☐
- comparison with competitors (benchmarking) ☐
- face-to-face interviews with existing customers ☐
- focus groups ☐
- motivational/psychological research ☐
- observation of consumer behaviour ☐

- questionnaires sent out through the post ☐
- statistics in government publications ☐
- statistics in specialized publications ☐
- study of more developed markets ☐
- telephone/street interviews ☐
- test marketing in a particular town/area ☐

2 Write notes about market research in your company.

Why?

Desk research

What? | How?

Field research

What? | How?

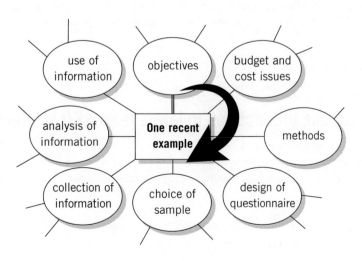

3 Discuss.

SALES AND MARKETING

Teacher's notes Sales and marketing: 15 Product design/R&D

15 Product design/R&D

Before you start

1 Are your students interested in this topic? Use the checklist on page 7.
2 Which classroom management options will you follow? See pages 4–5.
3 Do your students need language support for the discussions? See page 8.

1 Brainstorm issues to consider when you take a new product from R&D to full production.

1 Check comprehension of R&D (*Research and Development*). Focus attention on the flow chart and check vocabulary in the headings. (See *Vocabulary box* below.)

Vocabulary box

requirements: needs
specifications: technical requirements
design brief: a set of instructions for the design; the requirements/specifications will come mainly from the marketing department; the brief will include the *features:* main selling points of the product

prototype: first example of something that is used to test the design before full production; a prototype may not be fully functional.
set-up of machines: preparing the machines for production (also known as *tooling up* the machines)

2 Point out that the chart goes from left to right with two arrows pointing back to represent the need to redesign/make modifications because of a later stage. Get students to brainstorm vocabulary in pairs or small groups.
3 Elicit answers and write them on the board. (See *Possible answers/ideas* box below.)

Possible answers/ideas

Research issues: market research to find out consumer's needs (market research consists of both desk and field research, and uses questionnaires, discussion groups etc. See framework 14); availability of finance for R&D; control of budget; secrecy; lead time for the scientific research (*lead time:* the time between starting and finishing the research); conflict between scientific and commercial objectives; prioritizing different projects
Design issues: how the design brief is prepared; choice of designers (in-house or outsourced from another company); choice of design; limitations in the production technology available; designing for manufacture (simple designs that are easy to manufacture will lower production costs and

reduce defects); designing for recycling and easy disposal at the end of the product's life
Prototype issues: finding parts; problems in the construction of a working model; deciding how many working models to build
Consumer tests: how to choose the target group for the test; what geographical area to cover; what to measure in the tests; how to measure it
Production issues: supply of materials and parts; run time (the time it takes for a group of products manufactured together i.e. a *run* or *batch*, to go through the process); difficulties in estimating consumer demand. Also see frameworks 26 and 28 for more ideas.

Tip

Teach the following other useful terms:
setback: a problem that stops you making progress   *breakthrough:* an important new discovery

2 Write notes about one product you followed from R&D to production.

1 Get students to choose a product and make notes.
2 Circulate while students make notes. Write down on a piece of paper any useful language needed or produced. Write a few language items of general interest on the board at the end.

3 Discuss.

1 Which classroom management options will you follow? See pages 4–5.
2 Circulate during the discussion. Make a note of good/bad language use.

Feedback slot

See page 5.

Extension

- Students can write a short description of the product design/R&D process in their company.
- Consider repeating the activity in a later lesson e.g. with a different partner. See page 5.

38

15 Product design/R&D

1 Brainstorm issues to consider when you take a new product from R&D to full production.

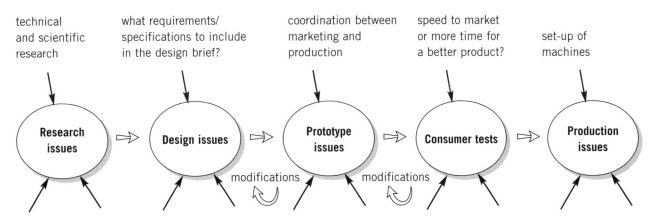

technical and scientific research

what requirements/ specifications to include in the design brief?

coordination between marketing and production

speed to market or more time for a better product?

set-up of machines

Research issues → Design issues → Prototype issues → Consumer tests → Production issues

modifications   modifications

2 Write notes about one product you followed from R&D to production.

Name of product: _____

Research issues

Design issues

Prototype issues

Consumer tests

Production issues

3 Discuss.

SALES AND MARKETING

16 Product description and features

1 Prepare.

Task 1

Get students to brainstorm more words and phrases to describe dimensions and shape. Write them on the board. (See *Possible answers/ideas* box below.)

Tip

Check pronunciation of *long/length*, *wide/width* and *high/height*. In particular, students often confuse *high* and *height*.

Possible answers/ideas

Size
It's 2 metres wide. It's 2 metres in width.
Its area is 2 square metres.
It's 2 metres high. It's 2 metres in height.
Its volume/capacity is 2 cubic metres.
It's 10 centimetres thick. It's 10 centimetres in thickness.

Weight
It's heavy/light.

Shape
Its shape is oval / rectangular / triangular / cylindrical / L-shaped.
It's in the shape of a …

Materials
It's made of steel / glass / cotton / polyester / wood / leather / rubber / synthetic materials / natural materials etc.

Task 2

1 Check comprehension of the word *feature* and of the vocabulary in the examples. (See *Vocabulary box* opposite.)
2 Get students to brainstorm more words and phrases to describe a product's features. Write them on the board. (See *Possible answers/ideas* box below.)

Vocabulary box

feature: an interesting and important part of a product that acts as a selling point. Students often use the word *characteristic* which is not so common in business and refers to a typical quality that makes something recognizable.

good value for money: this is often translated in other languages as 'a good relation between quality and price'. It is not the same as *cheap*, which refers only to price, or *economical*, which means 'using something carefully and without waste'.

reliable: something that rarely breaks down

Possible answers/ideas

- It's quiet / comfortable / easy to maintain / fast / portable / insulated / waterproof / environmentally friendly / resistant to corrosion / tailor-made/customized.
- It's got high-quality materials / a manual with clear instructions / a long active life / standard fixings.

Tip

Students may also need to talk about the technical specifications of their product, for example its speed, electricity/fuel consumption etc.

Task 3

Get students to complete the phrases with a few expressions. There is more space in section 2 for detailed comments. (No suggested answers are given here as it depends on the students' own products.)

2 Write notes about one of your company's products.

1 Focus attention on the ideas maps and check the vocabulary in the headings. Establish that students are going to describe a manufactured product that their company produces (existing or planned).
2 Circulate while students make notes. Write down on a piece of paper any useful language needed or produced. Write a few language items of general interest on the board at the end.

3 Give a mini-presentation. Ask for questions.

1 Explain that each student will give a mini-presentation to the class.
2 When it is their turn, let each student sit at the front and lead the session. Consider joining the group as a participant asking questions yourself, or sit away from the group. Make a note of good/bad language use.

Feedback slot

See page 5.

Extension

Students can write a short product presentation based on their notes and the speaking activity.

16 Product description and features

1 Prepare.

1 Brainstorm words and phrases to describe the size, weight, shape and materials of a product.

- It's 2 metres long. It's 2 metres in length.
- It weighs 2 kilos. It's 2 kilos in weight.
- Its shape is flat, curved, square, round, ...
- It's made of plastic, metal, ...

2 Brainstorm words and phrases to describe a product's *features* (selling points).

- It's modern, high quality, well-made, good value for money, efficient, easy to use, reliable, safe, available in a range of colours, long-lasting, user-friendly ...
- It's got an advanced design, the latest technology, low running costs, ...

3 Complete the phrases to talk about a product's *functions* (what it does).

- It solves all your ... problems.
- It allows you to ...
- It's used for ... (+ -*ing*)
- It can be tailor-made to ...

2 Write notes about one of your company's products.

Name of product: _____

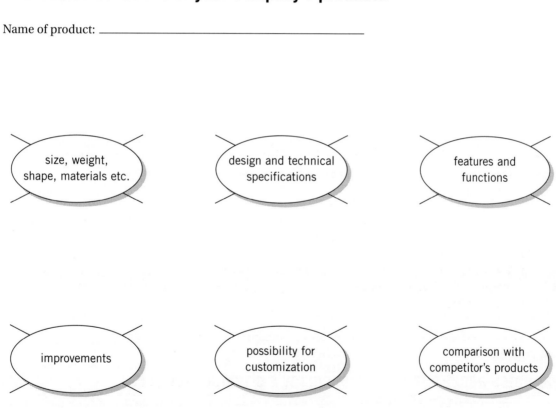

3 Give a mini-presentation. Ask for questions.

SALES AND MARKETING

17 Marketing mix: one product

Before you start

1 Are your students interested in this topic? Use the checklist on page 7.
2 Which classroom management options will you follow? See pages 4–5.
3 Do your students need language support for the discussions? See page 8.

1 Prepare.

1 Check comprehension of the instructions and get students to write the vocabulary in the correct columns. Then check the answers. (See *Vocabulary box* below if students need help with any of the items.)

Possible answers/ideas

Product: after-sales service, customer benefits, design, features/main selling points, launch, packaging (also could be in *Promotion*), quality, range

Price: demand in the market, discounts, value for money
Place: agent, availability, B2B, B2C, delivery, distribution channel, high street, retail outlet, shopping mall, wholesaler

Promotion: advertising, brochures/catalogues, cross-selling, trade fairs, mailshots, media, poster, sales force, special offer, sponsorship, word of mouth

Vocabulary box

Product
feature: an interesting and important part of a product that acts as a selling point. Students often use the word *characteristic* which is not so common in business and refers to a typical quality that makes something recognizable.
launch: to put a product on the market for the first time
range: a set of products of the same type
Price
demand: the amount that people are buying (price is largely determined by the balance between supply and demand)
value for money: giving good quality or a large amount considering the price

Place
availability: how easy it is to find/buy a product
B2B: business to business
B2C: business to consumer
high street: the main street of a town where many shops are (US = *main street*). The word is often used as a metaphor for retailing in general e.g. *high-street spending*.
retail outlet: any place where products are sold to the public e.g. supermarket, high-street shop, shopping mall, small corner shop, kiosk, vending machine etc.
Promotion
cross-selling: selling a product to existing customers who buy other products

mailshots: advertising material sent through the mail
media: all the ways of giving information and advertising to the public e.g. television, radio, magazines, newspapers, buses and taxis, posters etc.
sales force: all the people who sell the company's products
special offer: a reduction in the price of something for a short time, or a product/service that is added for a short time
sponsorship: financial support for a sports or arts event in exchange for advertising or public attention
word of mouth: when people hear about something from their friends

2 Check the vocabulary and get students to brainstorm other key questions. (No suggested answers are given here as they depend on individual products.)

2 Write notes about one of your company's products/services.

1 Focus attention on the grids and get students to choose a product/service. Ask them to answer some of the questions in section 1 task 2 in their notes.
2 Circulate while students make notes. Write down on a piece of paper any useful language needed or produced. Write a few language items of general interest on the board at the end.

3 Discuss.

1 Which classroom management options will you follow? See pages 4–5.
2 Circulate during the discussion. Make a note of good/bad language use.

Feedback slot

See page 5.

Extension

- Students can write a short summary of the marketing mix for their chosen product.
- Consider repeating the activity in a later lesson e.g. with a different partner. See page 5.

17 Marketing mix: one product

1 Prepare.

1 The marketing department creates a marketing mix for each product/service. This mix is often analysed using 'the 4 Ps'. On a separate piece of paper, divide the words and phrases in the box into four groups: Product, Price, Place, Promotion.

---

advertising   agent   after-sales service   availability   B2B   B2C   brochures/catalogues
cross-selling   customer benefits   delivery   demand in the market   design   discounts
distribution channel   features/main selling points   high street   launch   mailshots
media   packaging   poster   range   quality   retail outlet   sales force   shopping mall
special offer   sponsorship   trade fairs   value for money   wholesaler   word of mouth

---

2 Add key questions to the following lists.

Product issues

How was the product/service developed? What market research did you do? Are there production issues? What are the main selling points?

Price issues

How was the price decided: market demand? competitor's products? need for market share? other factors from the business plan?

Place issues

How do you decide where the product will be sold? What are the distribution channels? How could you improve them?

Promotion issues

How do you promote this product/service: TV? magazines? posters? Internet? mailshots? cross-selling? How did you decide on this mix of media?

2 Write notes about one of your company's products/services.

Name of product: _____

Product issues	Place issues
•	•
•	•

Price issues	Promotion issues
•	•
•	•

3 Discuss.

18 Marketing strategy

Before you start

1 Are your students interested in this topic? Use the checklist on page 7.
2 Which classroom management options will you follow? See pages 4–5.
3 Do your students need language support for the discussions? See page 8.

1 Prepare.

Task 1

1 Get students to brainstorm ideas in pairs or small groups.
2 Elicit answers and write them on the board.
(See *Possible answers/ideas* box below.)

Tip

Introduce a SWOT analysis very briefly at this stage, as preparation for the note-writing in section 2. Elicit the meanings of the four letters. See framework 13 for more information.

Possible answers/ideas

A marketing strategy might also depend on:
the ideas/vision of key people inside the company;
results of market research; feedback from sales reps e.g.
why certain products are selling well/badly etc.; the
human resources available; R&D activities of company;
changes in business environment (social, technological,
economic, political); the long-term strategy of the
company as defined by the board of directors etc.

Task 2

Get students to brainstorm ideas and write them on the board.

Tip

The list is already quite comprehensive, and if students can't think of any more items, move on quickly.

Task 3

1 Check students understand that the vocabulary items are all collocations with the word *market*.
Get students to fill in the missing vowels. Then check the answers. (See *Answers* box below.)

Answers

1 market *leader / niche / research / share / sector / segment / survey / trend*
2 to *target / enter / open up / capture / take over / withdraw from / be forced out of a* market

3 *a competitive / profitable / fragmented / saturated / growing / booming / stable / shrinking / volatile / specialized / domestic / international / worldwide / potential* market

2 Check comprehension of the vocabulary items. (See *Vocabulary box* below.)

Vocabulary box

market niche: a group of customers with particular needs (a niche is a small part of the market)
market sector/segment: a particular part of a market, e.g. a type of product or customer
market survey: a study of the state of the market
to target: to aim for
to withdraw from: to leave, to pull out of
fragmented: broken into many small parts

saturated: when all the possible customers have already bought the product, or when there is so much product for sale that there is more than people want
booming: growing rapidly
shrinking: declining
volatile: changing suddenly
potential: a possible future market

2 Write notes about the marketing strategy in your company.

1 Focus attention on the grids and check the vocabulary in the headings.
2 Circulate while students make notes. Write down on a piece of paper any useful language needed or produced. Write a few language items of general interest on the board at the end.

3 Discuss.

1 Which classroom management options will you follow? See pages 4–5.
2 Circulate during the discussion. Make a note of good/bad language use.

Feedback slot

See page 5.

Extension

- Students can write a short summary of the marketing strategy in their company.
- Consider repeating the activity in a later lesson e.g. with a different partner. See page 5.

18 Marketing strategy

1 Prepare.

1   A company's marketing strategy depends on many things. Brainstorm more ideas.

2   How can you differentiate your products from those of your competitors?
Add to the following list.

product features and design, price, availability and distribution, promotion, targeting different market sectors, ...

3   Fill in the missing vowels in these words and then check the meaning.

1   market   *l__d_r / n_ch_ / r_s__rch / sh_r_ / s_ct_r / s_gm_nt / s_rv_y / tr_nd*

2   to   *t_rg_t / _nt_r / _p_n   _p / c_pt_r_ / t_k_   _v_r / w_thdr_w   fr_m / b_   f_rc_d   __t   _f*   a market

3   a   *c_mp_t_t_v_ / pr_f_t_bl_ / fr_gm_nt_d / sat_r_t_d / gr_w_ng / b__ m_ng / st_bl_ / shr_nk_ng / v_l_t_l_ / sp_c__l_z_d / d_m_st_c / _nt_rn_t__n_l / w_rldw_d_ / p_t_nt__l*   market

2 Write notes about the marketing strategy in your company.

Strengths (good points about my company)	Weaknesses (bad points about my company)
Opportunities (future chances in the market)	**Threats** (future dangers in the market)

How do you differentiate your products/services from those of your competitors?

Future plans		
Sales targets. What? How?	**New products.** What? How?	**New markets.** What? How?

3 Discuss.

SALES AND MARKETING

19 Constraints on marketing strategy

Tip___
This framework is very much a follow-on from framework 18.

1 Read the text and check the vocabulary.

1 Get students to read the text and check the vocabulary. (See *Vocabulary box* below.)

Tip___
The text is quite comprehensive, but students at a higher level in the company who are used to thinking about marketing strategy might be able to think of more points not included here.

Vocabulary box ___

personnel: staff/employees
slowdown: when business activity is slower than before
recession: this is more serious than a *slowdown* and is defined as two consecutive quarters of negative growth in the economy

fluctuations: movements up and down
legislation: laws
lobbies: special interest groups who try to have an effect on government or company policy

2 Write notes.

Tasks 1 and 2

1 Focus attention on the ideas maps and check the vocabulary in the headings.
2 Circulate while students make notes. Write down on a piece of paper any useful language needed or produced. Write a few language items of general interest on the board at the end.

3 Discuss.

1 Which classroom management options will you follow? See pages 4–5.
2 Circulate during the discussion. Make a note of good/bad language use.

Feedback slot

See page 5.

Extension

- Students can write a short summary of the constraints on their marketing strategy.
- Consider repeating the activity in a later lesson e.g. with a different partner. See page 5.

19 Constraints on marketing strategy

1 Read the text and check the vocabulary.

A 'constraint' is something that limits or restricts your freedom of action. Constraints on a company's marketing strategy can be internal (inside the company) or external (outside the company).

Internal constraints include:

Financial constraints such as the size of your marketing budget and whether it is well spent.

Personnel constraints such as inexperienced staff.

Production constraints such as limits to your technology or production capacity.

Constraints due to your market position such as having a certain company image or a certain type of customer that limits your ability to move into new product areas or new markets.

External constraints include:

Competition, namely competitors' decisions about their own products, price, distribution channels and promotional activities.

Changes in the business environment often analysed in four 'STEP' factors: Society (social attitudes, consumer taste and fashion), Technology (new developments that make your products out of date), Economy (such as a slowdown or a recession, currency fluctuations, an increase in the cost of raw materials) and Politics (government policy, new legislation, activities of lobbies, international relations).

2 Write notes.

1 What are the constraints on your own company's marketing strategy?

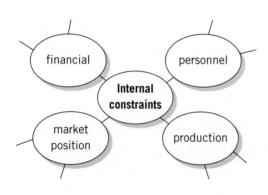
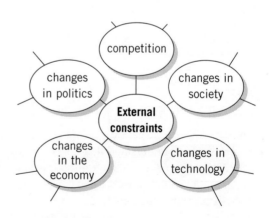

2 Choose three of the most important constraints. What plans are you making because of these constraints?

1 _____

_____

2 _____

_____

3 _____

_____

3 Discuss.

20 Marketing budget

Before you start

1 Are your students interested in this topic? Use the checklist on page 7.
2 Which classroom management options will you follow? See pages 4–5.
3 Do your students need language support for the discussions? See page 8.

Tip
Point out that *the marketing budget* is a detailed plan of how much a company will spend on marketing and what it will spend the money on.

1 Prepare.

Task 1

1 Focus attention on the ideas map and check the vocabulary in the headings. (See *Vocabulary box* below.)

Vocabulary box

media: all the ways of giving information and advertising
street posters: also called *hoardings* (US = *billboards*)
special offers: for example 2 for the price of 1, 10% free etc.
mailshots: advertising material sent through the mail
leaflet: a small piece of printed paper that gives information or advertises something
merchandising: the way in which goods are arranged in a store e.g. bottom/eye-level/top shelves, which products are put near to each other etc.

point-of-sale: the place where customers pay for something; *a point-of-sale display* would be on or near the checkout
sponsorship: financial support for a sports or arts event in exchange for advertising or public attention
endorsement: when a well-known person says how good something is or allows their name and image to be associated with the product

2 Get students to brainstorm ideas and write them on the board. (See *Possible answers/ideas* box below.)

Possible answers/ideas

media: radio; cinema; posters on the underground; posters on bus stops
special promotions: coupons in magazines; limited offers e.g. with better specifications or a special range of colours; give-away pens
printed materials: inserts inside magazines or other company's mail

in-store: free tasting; free samples
other: stands at trade fairs; telephone sales (including *cold calling* where the person is not yet a customer of the company and is not expecting the call); product placement in films or magazine articles, placing the logo on other company's products (e.g. on T-shirts); use of a slogan or piece of music that is easy to remember

Task 2

Get students to brainstorm ideas and write them on the board.

Task 3

1 Check students understand that the vocabulary items are all collocations related to the word *budget*. Get students to fill in the missing vowels. Then check the answers. (See *Answers* box opposite.)
2 Check comprehension of the vocabulary items. (See *Vocabulary box* opposite.)

Answers
to *draw up / set / spend / increase / reduce / exceed / keep within* a budget

Vocabulary box
to draw up: to think about and plan
to set: to decide what something should be
to exceed: to go beyond a limit
to keep within: not to go beyond a limit

2 Write notes.

Tasks 1 and 2

1 Focus attention on the grids and check the vocabulary in the headings.
2 Circulate while students make notes. Write down on a piece of paper any useful language needed or produced. Write a few language items of general interest on the board at the end.

3 Discuss.

1 Which classroom management options will you follow? See pages 4–5.
2 Circulate during the discussion. Make a note of good/bad language use.

Feedback slot

See page 5.

Extension

- Students can write a short report on how the marketing budget is spent in their company.
- Consider repeating the activity in a later lesson e.g. with a different partner. See page 5.

20 Marketing budget

1 Prepare.

1 What different types of promotion are there? Add to the ideas.

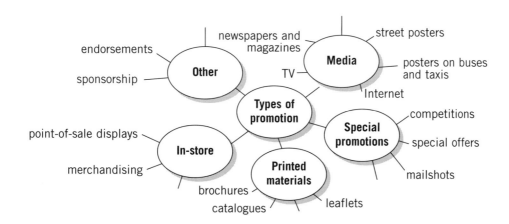

2 Apart from promotion, what other things might be paid for from the marketing budget? Add to the following list.

research and development of new products, market research, ...

3 Fill in the missing vowels in these words and then check the meaning.

to *dr_w / _p / s_t / sp_nd / _ncr_ _s_ / r_d_c_ / _xc__d / k__p w_th_n* a budget (for something)

2 Write notes.

1 Think about the marketing budget of your company.

Size of total budget
Who decides? How is the decision taken?

Choose four areas where you spend your marketing budget	
Who decides? How is the decision taken?	How do you measure the effectiveness of your spending?
1	
2	
3	
4	

2 Think of an example from your own experience where a marketing budget was used badly.

What happened?	Why?	Action taken?

3 Discuss.

21 Profit and loss account

FINANCE AND ACCOUNTING

Before you start
1 Are your students interested in this topic? Use the checklist on page 7.
2 Which classroom management options will you follow? See pages 4–5.
3 Do your students need language support for the discussions? See page 8.

Tip
A profit and loss (P&L) account is a document showing the amount of money earned and spent in a particular period.

1 Prepare.

Task 1

Get students to group the words. Then check the answers. (See *Answers* box below.)

Answers
turnover = revenue = sales
profit = earnings
reserves = retained profit

Tip
The word *income* is avoided in this framework because it has two meanings: sometimes a synonym of *turnover/revenue* and sometimes of *profit/earnings*. But note that in American English *Income statement* is used instead of *Profit and loss account*.

Task 2

Get students to match the words to the definitions. Then check the answers. (See *Answers* box below.)

Answers
amortization – 1 and 3
depreciation – 2

Tips
- Point out that the loss in value of an asset is taken away from a business's profits, so reducing the amount of tax to be paid.
- *Goodwill* is notoriously difficult to define, but is essentially the value of the existing customer base.

Task 3

Focus attention on the items in the P&L account. Get students to check the vocabulary. (See *Vocabulary box* below.) Then ask if it is presented in the same way in their company – usually it is very similar.

Vocabulary box

revenue: money obtained from customers for goods or services sold; *turnover* is also common
cost of goods sold: product-related costs such as raw materials, parts purchased, manufacturing expenses; also called *cost of sales*
gross: an amount before things have been taken away
rent: money paid to a landlord for the use of a building
utilities: electricity, gas and water
operating profit: the profit from the normal trading activities of the business

profit from investments: this might include money received by selling shares in other companies
exceptional item: an amount that is unlikely to be repeated e.g. capital gains received from the sale of assets or a part of the business
net: an amount after things have been taken away
retained profit: undistributed earnings; this money is available for reinvestment in the business
Other useful vocabulary
+ *plus,* – *minus,* = *equals*

2 Write notes.

1 Focus attention on the grids and check the vocabulary in the headings. (See *Vocabulary box* below.)

Vocabulary box

capital invested in the business: loan capital + share capital + retained profit. (See framework 22.)
the general state of the economy: this can be *stable,* in a *boom* or in *recession*

2 Circulate while students make notes. Write down on a piece of paper any useful language needed or produced. Write a few language items of general interest on the board at the end.

3 Discuss.

1 Which classroom management options will you follow? See pages 4–5.
2 Circulate during the discussion. Make a note of good/bad language use.

Feedback slot

See page 5.

Extension

Students can write a short summary of their company's P&L account issues, of those of their partner.

21 Profit and loss account

1 Prepare.

1 Put the words in the box into three groups with the same meaning.

| turnover | profit | reserves | earnings | revenue | sales | retained profit |

2 Write the word *amortization* or *depreciation* next to the correct definitions. One word is used twice.

1 the gradual loss in value of an intangible asset (like patents or goodwill) _____

2 the gradual loss in value of a fixed asset (like a building or a vehicle) _____

3 the gradual payment of a fixed asset or repayment of a loan _____

3 Study the profit and loss (P&L) account items below. Is a P&L account in your company presented in the same way?

```
Revenue
– Cost of goods sold (purchase of materials and parts, manufacturing costs etc.)

= Gross profit
– Operating expenses (salaries, rent, administration, selling and marketing expenses, utilities, R&D etc.)

= Operating profit
+ Profit from investments
+/– Exceptional items (one-time items e.g. the sale of an asset)

= Earnings before interest, tax, depreciation and amortization (EBITDA)
– Depreciation
– Amortization

= Earnings before interest and tax (EBIT)
+/– Interest (received from bank for cash balances or paid to bank for loans)

= Pre-tax earnings (= Profit before tax)
– Tax (paid to the government)

= Net earnings (= Profit after tax)
– Dividends (paid to shareholders)

= Retained profit
```

2 Write notes.

What are the important issues in your company at the moment in relation to the P&L account?		
What is your operating profit in relation to ...		
your competitors?	the capital invested in the business?	the general state of the economy?

3 Discuss.

22 Balance sheet

Before you start

1 Are your students interested in this topic? Use the checklist on page 7.
2 Which classroom management options will you follow? See pages 4–5.
3 Do your students need language support for the discussions? See page 8.

Tip
A balance sheet (BS) shows a picture of a business (what it owns and what it owes) at a specific point in time e.g. the last day of its financial year.

1 Prepare.

Task 1

Get students to cross out the wrong words. Then check the answers. (See *Answers* box opposite.)

Answers
Things that you own are called *assets* and things that you owe are *liabilities*.

Task 2

Get students to match the words and phrases with the definitions. Then check the answers. (See *Answers* box opposite.)

Answers
1b, 2a, 3c, 4f, 5d, 6e, 7h, 8g

Tip
See the Teacher's notes to framework 21 for notes on *goodwill*.

Task 3

Focus attention on the items in the BS. Get students to check the vocabulary. (See *Vocabulary box* below.) Then ask if it is presented in the same way in their company – usually it is very similar.

Vocabulary box

current assets: these are more 'liquid' than fixed assets i.e. they can be turned into cash more easily
inventory: raw materials + work in progress + finished goods
payable: due to be paid, but not paid yet
accrued: accumulated/built up gradually

payroll taxes: national insurance contributions payable, pension plans payable and redundancy payments payable
shareholders' equity: (also called *net assets/net worth*) the overall value of the business i.e. the amount to go to shareholders if the company sold all its assets and paid all its debts

Tip
Point out that the Profit and Loss Account reports what happened in a business between two BS dates e.g. over a year.

Task 4

Get students to complete the equation and discuss why working capital is important. Then check the answers. (See *Answers* box below.)

Answers
working capital = current assets – current liabilities
Companies need cash to operate the day-to-day business i.e. to pay salaries, suppliers and banks.
Working capital is a good indication of whether the company has enough cash to operate.

2 Write notes.

1 Focus attention on the grid and check the vocabulary in the headings. (See *Vocabulary box* opposite.)
2 Circulate while students make notes. Write down on a piece of paper any useful language needed or produced. Write a few language items of general interest on the board at the end.

Vocabulary box
CEO: Chief Executive Officer (UK = *Managing Director*)

3 Discuss.

1 Which classroom management options will you follow? See pages 4–5.
2 Circulate during the discussion. Make a note of good/bad language use.

Feedback slot

See page 5.

Extension

• Students can write a short summary of their company's BS issues, or those of their partner.

22 Balance sheet

1 Prepare.

1 Cross out the incorrect words in italics.

On a balance sheet (BS), things that you <u>own</u> are called *assets/liabilities* and things that you <u>owe</u> are called *assets/liabilities*.

2 Match the words and phrases (1–8) with the definitions (a–h).

1	fixed assets	**a**	assets that can be converted to cash within one year
2	current assets	**b**	assets that the company will use over a long time period
3	intangible assets	**c**	assets that are not physical and so cannot easily be valued e.g. copyrights, patents, franchises, goodwill, trade mark/brand name
4	loan capital		
5	share capital	**d**	money that has come into the company from issuing shares
6	retained profit	**e**	money that has come into the company from its operations
7	accounts receivable	**f**	money that has come into the company from bank loans
8	accounts payable	**g**	money owed to suppliers (= *creditors*)
		h	money owed by customers (= *debtors*)

3 Study the balance sheet items below. Is a BS in your company presented in the same way?

Current assets Cash Accounts receivable Inventory (raw materials and stock) Shares intended for disposal within 1 year **Fixed assets** Vehicles and equipment Investments (= *financial assets*) Land and buildings **Intangible assets** Goodwill (of companies you have bought), patents etc.	**Current liabilities** Loan capital (= *bank debt*) Accounts payable Accrued expenses (other items not yet paid e.g. unpaid utility bills, unpaid payroll taxes) Tax payable (tax on operating profit) **Provisions** Amount set aside for future liabilities (e.g. writing off a bad debt, restructuring costs, a court case) **Shareholders' equity** Share capital Retained profit (= *reserves*)

4 Complete this equation using phrases from the BS. Then answer the question.

working capital = _____ – _____

Why is working capital important to a business?

2 Write notes.

What are the important issues in your company at the moment in relation to the BS?
What is your company doing to decrease the tax payable?
What plans do you think the Board of Directors or CEO have to improve the BS next year?

3 Discuss.

23 Managing cashflow

Before you start

1 Are your students interested in this topic? Use the checklist on page 7.
2 Which classroom management options will you follow? See pages 4–5.
3 Do your students need language support for the discussions? See page 8.

1 Brainstorm.

Task 1

1 Focus attention on the ideas maps and check the vocabulary in the headings. (See *Vocabulary box* below.)

Vocabulary box

cashflow: the cash coming into, or being paid out by, the business. The difference between *cash* and *profit* is timing. Many profitable businesses run out of cash if they do not collect it quickly enough or if they spend it too quickly. If so, they have liquidity problems (inability to pay bills and loans). The term *working capital* is often used as a synonym for *cashflow.* (See framework 22.)

chase debtors: try hard to get money from people who owe it to you e.g. by writing reminder letters, making phone calls etc.
stock control: this includes control of raw materials + WIP (work in progress) + finished goods
bank facilities: this includes both overdrafts (temporary negative balances on your bank account where you go *into the red* for a short time) and short-term loans

2 Get students to brainstorm vocabulary in pairs or small groups.
3 Elicit answers and write them on the board. (See *Possible answers/ideas* box below.)

Possible answers/ideas

Causes of cashflow problems: marketing problems such as generous credit being offered to try to sell unsold stocks; lower demand due to slowdown in the economy/competitors' products entering the market/changes in fashion or season; unexpected non-payments by customers (= *bad debts*)
Increasing cashflow by credit control: review credit of existing customers; make payments to suppliers in

several instalments i.e. 'stage' the payments, reduce spending on fixed assets e.g. lease rather than buy equipment
Increasing cashflow by stock control: minimize stock losses; minimize work-in-progress (WIP); deliver to customers quickly
Increasing cashflow by reducing payments: delay spending on capital equipment

Task 2

Elicit other ways to increase cashflow. (See *Possible answers/ideas* box below.)

Possible answers/ideas

Marketing initiatives to increase sales and generate cash quickly e.g. special promotions, reduced prices; factoring (paying an outside company to recover the debt); cutting costs in specific areas; selling assets

2 Write notes.

Tasks 1 and 2

1 Focus attention on the questions and on the grid and check the vocabulary.
2 Circulate while students make notes. Write down on a piece of paper any useful language needed or produced. Write a few language items of general interest on the board at the end.

3 Discuss.

1 Which classroom management options will you follow? See pages 4–5.
2 Circulate during the discussion. Make a note of good/bad language use.

Feedback slot

See page 5.

Extension

- Students can write a short summary of their own cashflow management, or that of their partner.
- Consider repeating the activity in a later lesson e.g. with a different partner. See page 5.

23 Managing cashflow

1 Brainstorm.

1 Complete the ideas maps.

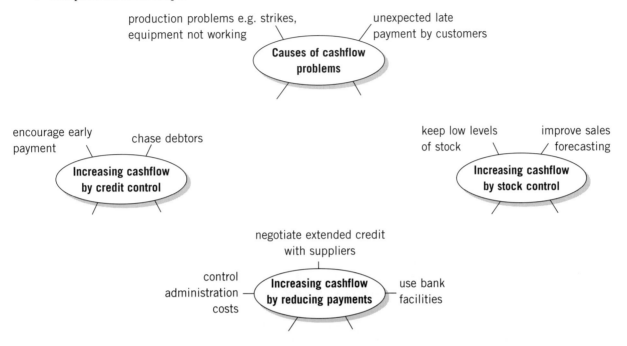

production problems e.g. strikes, equipment not working

unexpected late payment by customers

Causes of cashflow problems

encourage early payment

chase debtors

Increasing cashflow by credit control

keep low levels of stock

improve sales forecasting

Increasing cashflow by stock control

negotiate extended credit with suppliers

control administration costs

Increasing cashflow by reducing payments

use bank facilities

2 What other ways are there to increase cashflow?

2 Write notes.

1 What causes cashflow problems in your business? Give three real-life examples.

1 _____

2 _____

3 _____

2 How do you try to solve cashflow problems? What problems does this cause?

Methods we use to improve cashflow	Problems associated with these methods
1	⇨
2	⇨
3	⇨

3 Discuss.

24 Company analysis

Before you start

1 Are your students interested in this topic? Use the checklist on page 7.
2 Which classroom management options will you follow? See pages 4–5.
3 Do your students need language support for the discussions? See page 8.

Tip

This framework is particularly suitable for investment/financial analysts, as it gets students to do a market and financial analysis on a company that they have recently studied. The framework leads to a recommendation about whether or not to invest in the company. Students could also use this framework to analyse their own company.

1 What do you need to know about a company to analyse its current performance and future potential? Brainstorm.

1 Focus attention on the ideas maps and check the vocabulary in the headings. (See *Vocabulary box* below.)

Vocabulary box

reputation of senior executives: this means reputation amongst fund managers, analysts, journalists etc.
unique competitive advantages: these include brands, patents, copyrights, designs, technology etc.

Tip

See frameworks 22 and 23 for further information on items in the *Financial information* section.

2 Get students to brainstorm vocabulary in pairs or small groups.
3 Elicit answers and write them on the board. (See *Possible answers/ideas* box below.)

Possible answers/ideas

Background information
How long has the business been running? What is its track record (past performance)? Has the company grown organically or by acquisitions? What is the success of different divisions/subsidiaries? Is the market fragmented or do a few big companies dominate? What are the barriers to entry for start-up companies?

Product/service information
Are the products/services long-life or will they have to change rapidly?

Financial information
Who are the major shareholders? How liquid (easy to buy and sell) are the shares? Is the price/earnings (p/e) ratio

reasonable compared to other similar companies? (A high p/e ratio in comparison to other similar companies means that the shares are expensive and in demand with investors, perhaps because the company has good long-term growth prospects.) Is the yield attractive compared to other similar companies (*yield:* the dividend paid per share expressed as a percentage of the price of the share – a high yield means that the company is making good profits and returning these to shareholders)? Is the company vulnerable to currency fluctuations? (Would it be harmed by a big change in e.g. the value of the dollar against the euro?) Is the company vulnerable to commodity price movements (movements in the cost of oil and other raw materials)?

2 Write notes.

Tasks 1 and 2

1 Focus attention on the questions and grids and check the vocabulary.

Tip

Remind students that they are going to analyse a real company that they know about or have recently studied.

2 Circulate while students make notes. Write down on a piece of paper any useful language needed or produced. Write a few language items of general interest on the board at the end.

3 Discuss.

1 Which classroom management options will you follow? See pages 4–5.
2 Circulate during the discussion. Make a note of good/bad language use.

Feedback slot

See page 5.

Extension

- Students can write a short report on their chosen company.
- Consider repeating the activity in a later lesson e.g. with a different partner. See page 5.

24 Company analysis

1 What do you need to know about a company to analyse its current performance and future potential? Brainstorm.

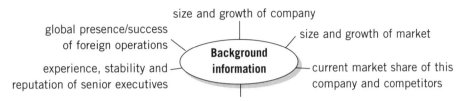

size and growth of company

global presence/success of foreign operations

Background information

size and growth of market

experience, stability and reputation of senior executives

current market share of this company and competitors

main products/services   main customers

mix of different product areas

Product/service information

any unique competitive advantages

turnover + trend   operating profit + trend

recent performance of share price

Financial information

cashflow

balance sheet issues: assets and debt

2 Write notes.

1 Choose a company you have recently analysed and complete the grids.

Name of company: _____

Background information
•   •   •   •

Product/service information
•   •   •   •

Financial information
•   •   •   •

2 Would you recommend this company to investors? Give three main reasons.

1 _____

2 _____

3 _____

3 Discuss.

FINANCE AND ACCOUNTING

25 Investment advice

Before you start

1 Are your students interested in this topic? Use the checklist on page 7.
2 Which classroom management options will you follow? See pages 4–5.
3 Do your students need language support for the discussions? See page 8.

1 Prepare.

Task 1

Get students to read the text and underline any words they don't recognize. (See *Vocabulary box* below.)

Vocabulary box

stocks: a share in the value of a company. *Stocks* is more usual in American English; *shares* is used only in British English. When you buy stocks in a company you own part of the company; stocks can rise and fall in value and be sold at a profit or loss, and they also pay a regular dividend to the holder.
equities: a more technical term for *stocks*
bond: a document issued by a company or government that says that a loan will be repaid at a certain date and will pay a fixed rate of interest to the holder until then.

Bonds are long-term investments and the bond itself can be bought and sold.
to diversify a portfolio: to increase the variety of investments that you have
return: profit in this context
funds: this is a general word. In British English there are *unit trusts* and *investment trusts*; in American English there are *mutual funds*. *Domestic funds* are funds invested in a person's own national stock market.

Tip

There are other investment instruments such as *derivatives* (betting on future stock prices), *money market funds* (funds made up of short-term loans to companies), art and antiques etc. If students mention these, ask them to say if they are short- or long-term investments and if they are high or low risk.

Task 2

1 Check students understand that the vocabulary items are all collocations related to investments. Get students to fill in the missing vowels. Then check the answers. (See *Answers* box opposite.)
2 Check comprehension of the vocabulary items. (See *Vocabulary box* below.)

Answers

1 a *poor / low / acceptable / competitive / fixed / good / high / current* rate of interest
2 a *negative / uncertain / bright / healthy / positive* outlook for the market
3 a *high / medium / low* level of *risk/return* in the *short / medium / long* term

Vocabulary box

outlook: what is expected to happen in the future; *outlook* is more common in business than the word *prediction*.
risk vs. *return:* all investments involve a balance between risk and return.

2 A client has $50,000 to invest for long-term growth. This client has no other investments. Prepare some advice. Write notes.

1 Focus attention on the grids and check the vocabulary in the headings. Establish that students are going to imagine that they are giving investment advice to a client from their own country, and that the client wants long-term growth (i.e. not income) and has no other investments.
2 Circulate while students make notes. Write down on a piece of paper any useful language needed or produced. Write a few language items of general interest on the board at the end.

3 Discuss.

1 Which classroom management options will you follow? See pages 4–5.
2 Circulate during the discussion. Make a note of good/bad language use.

Feedback slot

See page 5.

Extension

- Students can write a report with recommendations for their client.
- Consider repeating the activity in a later lesson e.g. with a different partner. See page 5.

25 Investment advice

1 Prepare.

1 Read the text and check the vocabulary.

Investment instruments include stocks (equities), bonds and cash. Most investors like to have a diversified portfolio of all three. Stocks offer a higher potential return over the long term, but at a higher risk. Bonds offer a fixed rate of interest, and have less risk. They can be issued by governments (in which case they are called gilts), or companies. Cash sits in a bank account earning interest. It is the safest investment, but offers the lowest returns.

Instead of investing in individual stocks, investors can spread their risk by investing in funds. These can be geographical funds (domestic/regional/international), sector funds (e.g. the technology/financial/health care/retail sectors), tracker funds (that 'track' or follow exactly a stock market index such as the S&P 500), emerging market funds or small company funds.

2 Fill in the missing vowels in these words and then check the meaning.

1 a *p_ _r / l_w / _cc_pt_bl_ / c_mp_t_t_v_ / f_x_d / g_ _d / h_gh / c_rr_nt* rate of interest

2 a *n_g_t_v_ / _nc_rt_ _n / br_ght / h_ _lthy / p_s_t_v_* outlook for the market

3 a *h_gh / m_d_ _m / l_w* level of *r_sk / r_t_rn* in the *sh_rt / m_d_ _m / l_ng* term

2 A client has $50,000 to invest for long-term growth. This client has no other investments. Prepare some advice. Write notes.

Market background and outlook
My national stock market
Other national stock markets
Sectors with a positive outlook
Outlook for bonds

Suggested % split between instruments + reasons			
Domestic equities ...... %	International & specialized equities ...... %	Fixed interest ...... %	Cash deposits ...... %

Equity part of investment: which stocks/funds/regions/sectors? + reasons

Fixed interest part of investment: which bonds/funds? + reasons

3 Discuss.

26 Production process

1 Prepare.

Task 1

1 Focus attention on the ideas maps and check the vocabulary in the headings. (See *Vocabulary box* below.)

Vocabulary box

variation of output: how different each manufactured item will be, and how that difference is achieved

customization: changing the product according to the customer's requirements

sourcing: sourcing and *procurement* are wider terms than *purchasing*. They refer to establishing supply chains for inputs to the production process as well as ordering and negotiating the price.

WIP: work in progress

stock control: control of raw materials + WIP + finished goods

minimizing: keeping to a minimum; this is important as a low level of stock means better cashflow

run time: the time it takes for a group of products manufactured together to go through the process

set-ups: preparing the machines for production i.e. tooling and retooling the machines

maintenance: keeping something in good condition; *repair* is fixing something that is broken or damaged

2 Get students to brainstorm vocabulary in pairs or small groups.
3 Elicit answers and write them on the board. (See *Possible answers/ideas* box below.)

Possible answers/ideas

Planning issues: minimizing the number of set-ups, minimizing stock levels; scheduling (general planning e.g. raw materials/day, units produced/day); CAD/CAM

Sourcing issues: subcontracting/contracting out/ outsourcing (employing other companies to make certain components); maintaining continuity of supply; delivery speed; flexibility of supplier; quality control of materials and parts; negotiating with suppliers

Stock control issues: minimizing stock losses; checking the expiry date of stocks

Production issues: quality control (see framework 28); labour skill required; automation/robotics; build quality (high/low quality of the manufacturing); production problems (e.g. strikes, equipment not working); packing and dispatch; transport and delivery

Task 2

Get students to explain the terms 1–5 and give examples. (See *Answers* box below.)

Answers

1 Single-item production is a unique product which is made to order and produced at the producer's premises e.g. a made-to-measure suit.

2 Batch production is the manufacture of different versions of the same basic product in small groups e.g. different colours of paint, flavours of yoghurt.

3 Line production is the manufacture of a standard product on an assembly line e.g. motor vehicles.

4 Continuous flow production is where machinery produces a single, standard product on a 24-hour basis e.g. chemical manufacture or oil refining.

5 An on-site project is a unique product assembled on site e.g. a ship or a civil engineering project.

2 Write notes.

Tasks 1 and 2

1 Focus attention on the grid and check the vocabulary in the headings.
2 Circulate while students make notes. Write down on a piece of paper any useful language needed or produced. Write a few language items of general interest on the board at the end.

3 Discuss.

1 Which classroom management options will you follow? See pages 4–5.
2 Circulate during the discussion. Make a note of good/bad language use.

Feedback slot

See page 5.

26 Production process

1 Prepare.

1 Brainstorm issues in the production process.

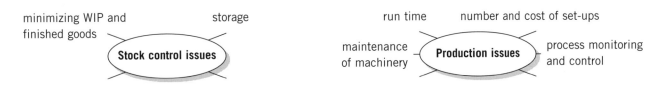

2 Explain the following terms and give examples.

1 single-item production   3 line production   5 an on-site project
2 batch production   4 continuous flow production

2 Write notes.

1 Draw a flow chart of the production process that you use.

2 Write notes about your production process.

Planning issues	Sourcing issues
•	•
•	•
Stock control issues	Production issues
•	•
•	•

3 Discuss.

PRODUCTION AND OPERATIONS

27 Operations growth

Before you start
1 Are your students interested in this topic? Use the checklist on page 7.
2 Which classroom management options will you follow? See pages 4–5.
3 Do your students need language support for the discussions? See page 8.

1 Brainstorm.

1 Focus attention on the ideas maps and check the vocabulary in the headings. (See *Vocabulary box* below.)

Tip

Teach higher-level students the phrase *economies of scale* – a synonym of *cost benefits of growth*.

Vocabulary box

bulk buying: buying in large quantities

better utilization of capacity: increasing production using the same machinery, thereby lowering the cost per unit

reduced risk: this is because a diversified and expanded product range means the company is less dependent on a few main products

managerial specialization: this should improve the quality of decision-making

management communication problems: these include more complex lines of communication, less direct personal feedback to top management, difficulty in coordinating and delegating etc.

plant: a factory and all its equipment; the problem with running at full capacity is that you might have to refuse some business, and maintenance could be difficult

2 Get students to brainstorm vocabulary in pairs or small groups.
3 Elicit answers and write them on the board. (See *Possible answers/ideas* box below.)

Possible answers/ideas

Cost benefits of growth: opportunities for financial savings e.g. borrowing money more easily and at lower rates of interest; opportunities to invest in newer, more efficient technology and machinery

Other benefits of growth: opportunities to use the salesforce more efficiently – perhaps a similar number of sales staff can sell a wider range of goods or produce a higher volume of turnover; opportunities to use labour more efficiently e.g. specialization in the factory

Problems of growth: human resource problems e.g. staff turnover/training/stress etc.; general loss of control; general loss of the flexibility that a smaller company has

2 Write notes about the growth in operations in your company.

1 Focus attention on the grids and check the vocabulary in the headings.
2 Circulate while students make notes. Write down on a piece of paper any useful language needed or produced. Write a few language items of general interest on the board at the end.

Tip

Use the following prompts if the students have problems getting started:
Why are you growing?
Reasons could include internal growth i.e. increasing sales, or external growth e.g. entering into a joint venture (a business activity in which two or more companies are working together on an individual project or in a particular market), a merger (when two companies join) or an acquisition (when one company buys another, also called a *takeover*).
What is the impact of growth on other departments?
Examples include purchasing economies, marketing economies, financial economies etc.

3 Discuss.

1 Which classroom management options will you follow? See pages 4–5.
2 Circulate during the discussion. Make a note of good/bad language use.

Feedback slot
See page 5.

Extension
• Students can write a short report on the positive and negative effects of the growth in operations in their company.
• Consider repeating the activity in a later lesson e.g. with a different partner. See page 5.

27 Operations growth

1 Brainstorm.

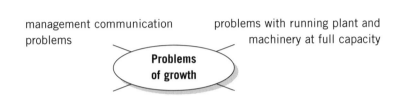

2 Write notes about the growth in operations in your company.

Background	
Why are you growing?	**How are you growing?**

Benefits	
Cost benefits • • •	**Other benefits** • • •

Problems	Possible solutions
1	⇨
2	⇨
3	⇨

What is the impact of growth on other departments?

3 Discuss.

PRODUCTION AND OPERATIONS

28 Quality management

Before you start
1 Are your students interested in this topic? Use the checklist on page 7.
2 Which classroom management options will you follow? See pages 4–5.
3 Do your students need language support for the discussions? See page 8.

1 Read the text and check the vocabulary. Do you agree with the paragraph on the right?

Get students to read the text and underline any words they don't recognize. (See *Vocabulary box* below.) Then discuss if students agree with the final paragraph.

Tip

Students who are involved in quality management might mention quality certificates like ISO 9000, 9001, 9002 etc. Ask them what they had to do to get their certificate, what benefits it brings, and what they have to do to keep their certificate.

Vocabulary box

waste: unwanted materials that are left after a particular process

sample: a small amount that is examined in order to find out what the rest is like

defects: faults in the way something is made

damage: physical harm to something so that it is broken

set-up time: the time it takes to prepare machinery for production

lead time: a general business word for the time it takes to do something, here meaning the time it takes to make a product after receiving the order

stock: raw materials + parts/components + WIP (work in progress) + finished goods; (US = *inventory*)

Just-In-Time (JIT): a method of planning production and stock control where the smallest possible amount of raw materials and WIP are held. This means planning for the inputs for each stage in the process to arrive only at the time they are needed. JIT means that production only takes place when there is an actual customer order.

Tip

Another technique in TQM is *benchmarking*, which means using the performance of an excellent company as a standard to judge and improve other companies. If students mention this, ask them to give examples of their experience of benchmarking.

2 Write notes.

Tasks 1 and 2

1 Focus attention on the ideas map and check the vocabulary in the headings.
2 Circulate while students make notes. Write down on a piece of paper any useful language needed or produced. Write a few language items of general interest on the board at the end.

Tip

The problems referred to in task 2 will be from the students' own companies, but typical examples include inspection costs, training costs, costs of changes to production methods, the time required to make the quality initiatives work, any difficulties persuading shareholders and others to take a long-term view etc.

3 Discuss.

1 Which classroom management options will you follow? See pages 4–5.
2 Circulate during the discussion. Make a note of good/bad language use.

Feedback slot

See page 5.

Extension

- Students can write a short report on quality management in their company.
- Consider repeating the activity in a later lesson e.g. with a different partner. See page 5.

28 Quality management

1 Read the text and check the vocabulary. Do you agree with the paragraph on the right?

Total quality management (TQM) is a management philosophy with Japanese origins. It aims to improve quality and to reduce waste, inefficiency and unnecessary costs in the manufacturing process. This can be done:

- at the design stage, for example integrating design and engineering so that the design ideas are easy to manufacture.
- by inspection and detection, for example traditional quality control techniques such as visual checks, taking samples, testing etc.
- by improving the production process itself, for example minimizing waste, faults/defects, damage, set-up times, lead times.
- by stock control, for example keeping low inventory levels (including raw materials, parts, components, work-in-progress and finished goods) or trying to organize production around specific customer orders (Just-In-Time techniques).
- by involving suppliers, for example looking for more flexible (or reliable) delivery times.
- by involving staff, for example asking workers to suggest improvements to working practices, training them to detect and correct faults, training them to be flexible and multi-skilled.

TQM was very popular in the 1980s, but nowadays it is less fashionable. There are three main reasons for this. Firstly, the lessons have been learned and quality in manufacturing these days is usually good. Secondly, the theory was difficult to apply in the service and information sectors of the economy. Thirdly, TQM initiatives did not always lead to profitability and success: they were important operationally but long-term success was – and is – much more to do with company strategy.

2 Write notes.

1 What initiatives are you taking to improve quality in your products and reduce waste, inefficiency and costs in the production process? Complete the ideas map.

2 What problems are associated with these quality initiatives? What are the possible solutions?

3 Discuss.

PRODUCTION AND OPERATIONS

29 Logistics and transport

Before you start

1 Are your students interested in this topic? Use the checklist on page 7.
2 Which classroom management options will you follow? See pages 4–5.
3 Do your students need language support for the discussions? See page 8.

1 Prepare.

Task 1

Discuss the question briefly as a class and elicit a range of definitions. (See *Possible answer* box opposite.)

Possible answer

logistics – the practical arrangements necessary so that the right things are in the right place at the right time

Task 2

1 Put students in pairs and get them to discuss the difference between the items in numbers 1–12. Make sure that students understand that for some items there is no difference.
2 Check the answers with the whole class. (See *Answers* box below.)

Answers

1 *goods:* things that are produced; *freight/cargo:* goods carried on a ship, plane, truck or train
2 *a factory:* a building where goods are produced in large quantities; *a warehouse:* a large building used for storing goods in large quantities
3 *a van:* a vehicle used for carrying goods which has metal sides and is smaller than a truck; *a truck:* a large vehicle used for carrying heavy loads; *a lorry* is the British English term for *a truck*
4 *a port:* a town where ships can stop; *a dock:* the part of a port where the ship ties up and goods are taken on and off
5 *to load:* to put goods on or into a vehicle; *to unload:* to take goods off or out of a vehicle
6 *a batch:* a quantity of goods produced at the same time; *a consignment:* a quantity of goods sent at the same time

7 *returned goods:* goods that the customer sends back because they are wrong, damaged or unwanted; *reissued goods:* goods sent to replace the returned goods
8 *to dispatch:* to send goods out from where they are produced or stored; *to track:* to follow the progress of the goods while they are being transported; *to deliver:* to take goods to their final destination
9 *to handle goods:* to deal with them or to touch/hold them; *to handle a complaint:* to deal with it
10 *a distributor:* a company that supplies goods to shops and companies; *an agent:* a person or company who represents another person's business; *a broker:* a person who buys and sells stocks, property, etc. for others
11 *to fulfil an order:* to supply what has been ordered; *to fulfil a requirement:* to provide what is needed
12 *en route* and *in transit* (no difference): on the way

Task 3

1 Get students to brainstorm the advantages and disadvantages of each mode of transport in pairs or small groups.
2 Elicit answers and write them on the board. (See *Possible answers* box below.)

Possible answers

Road transport	Rail transport	Air transport	Sea transport
Advantages: door-to-door service, flexible timetable, simple, can reach everywhere Disadvantages: traffic	Advantages: cheap, good for containers and large quantities Disadvantages: routes limited by railways	Advantages: fast over long distances Disadvantages: weight and size of cargo limited, expensive	Advantages: cheap, good for containers and large quantities Disadvantages: very slow

2 What are current issues related to logistics in your business? Write notes.

1 Focus attention on the grid and check the vocabulary in the headings.
2 Circulate while students make notes. Write down on a piece of paper any useful language needed or produced. Write a few language items of general interest on the board at the end.

3 Discuss.

1 Which classroom management options will you follow? See pages 4–5.
2 Circulate during the discussion. Make a note of good/bad language use.

Feedback slot

See page 5.

29 Logistics and transport

1 Prepare.

1 Think of a good definition for *logistics*.

_____

2 What is the difference between the words and phrases in the following sets?

1 *goods* and *freight/cargo*	7 *returned goods* and *reissued goods*
2 *a factory* and *a warehouse*	8 *to dispatch, to track* and *to deliver* an order
3 *a van, a truck* and *a lorry*	9 *to handle goods* and *to handle a complaint*
4 *a port* and *a dock*	10 *a distributor, an agent* and *a broker*
5 *to load* and *to unload*	11 *to fulfil a customer's order* and *to fulfil a customer's requirements*
6 *a batch* and *a consignment*	12 *en route* and *in transit*

3 Brainstorm.

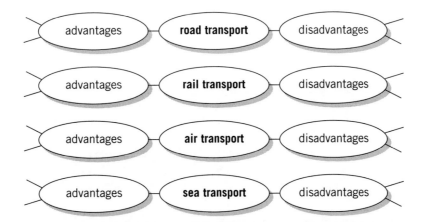

2 What are current issues related to logistics in your business? Write notes.

Logistics and ...	Main issues	Changes needed/future plans
sourcing/ purchasing		
storage/ warehousing		
choice of transport		
the distribution channel (different stages, people involved etc.)		
customer services (returning and reissuing goods etc.)		

3 Discuss.

30 Pay and promotion

Before you start

1 Are your students interested in this topic? Use the checklist on page 7.
2 Which classroom management options will you follow? See pages 4–5.
3 Do your students need language support for the discussions? See page 8.

1 Check the vocabulary and add examples.

1 Check the vocabulary with the whole class. (See *Vocabulary box* below.)

Vocabulary box

salary: this is now a close synonym for *pay* and *wages*, but originally *salary* meant monthly pay to a bank account for white-collar workers and *wages* meant weekly pay in cash to blue-collar workers; *wages* is still a more common usage for factory workers.

level/position: place in the company hierarchy

length of service: time in the company

qualifications: academic examinations that you have passed e.g. university degree, MBA

bonus: an extra amount of money added to an employee's salary as a reward for increasing sales/profits or cutting costs, usually done on an individual basis

appraisal interview: a regular (usually annual) meeting between an employee, his/her line manager and perhaps other managers e.g. from Human Resources (HR), where the employee's work over the year is appraised i.e. discussed in terms of how valuable, effective and successful it has been. This meeting is an opportunity to discuss strengths and weaknesses, achievements, targets, performance-related pay, bonuses, training and promotion etc.

profit-sharing scheme: when a company gives part of its profits to its employees, usually done on a company-wide basis

stock options: the right to buy shares in the company at a fixed price after working for a certain period of time. The employee can then sell those shares and make a profit if the market price at the time is higher (usually offered to senior managers as an incentive to increase the share price).

benefits: these are also known as *perks* and *fringe benefits*, although the latter two terms are less common nowadays in the HR context as they suggest that the benefits are of little importance

company pension plan: payments into a fund that will give the employee an increased pension when they retire, in addition to the basic state pension

private health insurance: medical insurance that allows you to use a private hospital if you become ill

promotion: moving to a better, more responsible position at work

2 Get students to add examples to the lists. This depends very much on the students' own companies, but see the *Possible answers/ideas* box below for other benefits.

Possible answers/ideas

Other benefits: entertainment allowance (a sum of money that you are given to spend on taking customers to restaurants etc.); relocation expenses (to help you move to a new area to work); subsidized canteen (a place where employees can eat cheaply); sports club membership; discount on the company's own goods; training

2 Write notes on how you make decisions about pay and promotion.

1 Focus attention on the grids and check the vocabulary in the headings. Point out that there is space for students to describe and evaluate a real-life example in each area (a mini case study).
2 Circulate while students make notes. Write down on a piece of paper any useful language needed or produced. Write a few language items of general interest on the board at the end.

3 Discuss.

1 Which classroom management options will you follow? See pages 4–5.
2 Circulate during the discussion. Make a note of good/bad language use.

Feedback slot

See page 5.

Extension

- Ask students how their own pay is decided.
- Students can write a short summary of the pay and promotion policy in their company.
- Consider repeating the activity in a later lesson e.g. with a different partner. See page 5.

30 Pay and promotion

1 Check the vocabulary and add examples.

1 **Basic salary issues:** level/position in the company, length of service, qualifications,

_____

2 **Performance-related pay issues:** a bonus based on results, individual or team results, an appraisal interview, a profit-sharing scheme, stock options for senior managers,

_____

3 **Benefits:** company pension plan, private health insurance, company car, credit card, laptop computer, mobile phone, childcare facilities, transport to the workplace,

_____

4 **Promotion issues:** What opportunities are available? Who else is interested in the same job? What is the career objective of the individual person?

_____

2 Write notes on how you make decisions about pay and promotion.

| Decision process for basic salary | Example |
| | Evaluation of this case |

| Decision process for performance-related pay | Example |
| | Evaluation of this case |

| Decision process for benefits | Example |
| | Evaluation of this case |

| Decision process for promotion | Example |
| | Evaluation of this case |

3 Discuss.

HUMAN RESOURCES

31 Motivation through job satisfaction

1 Read the text and check the vocabulary.

Get students to read the text and underline any words they don't recognize. (See *Vocabulary box* below.)

Tip
> You can return to the questions in the text and ask and answer them in class. This will not affect section 2, as the questions are quite general and the framework boxes ask the students to give specific examples.

Vocabulary box

lines of communication: communication between senior managers, middle managers, junior managers and non-managerial staff/front-line staff/workers

regular feedback: giving advice or suggestions for improvement, or telling people how good their work is

appraisal process: a regular (usually annual) interview between an employee, his/her line manager and perhaps other managers, e.g. from Human Resources (HR), where the employee's work over the year is appraised i.e. discussed in terms of how valuable, effective and successful it has been – this meeting is an opportunity to discuss strengths and weaknesses, achievements, targets met or not met, targets for next year, performance-related pay, bonuses, opportunities for training and promotion etc.

to involve people: to include them, to make them feel they are necessary; *involvement* (n)

to achieve: to complete a task by hard work and skill; *achievement* (n)

to delegate: to give work or responsibilities to somebody in a lower position; *delegation* (n)

appropriate: suitable or right for the situation

committed: willing to work hard; *commitment* (n)

loyal: faithful in your support of something; *loyalty* (n)

morale: the level of confidence and hope for the future that the employees feel

level of sickness: how many people do not come to work because they are ill

staff turnover: how many people leave the company and need to be replaced

grievance: an official complaint about unfair behaviour (but before the issue becomes, for example, a strike)

2 Write notes about your company.

1 Focus attention on the grids and check the vocabulary in the headings. Point out that in some boxes students are asked to describe and evaluate a real-life example (a case study).

2 Circulate while students make notes. Write down on a piece of paper any useful language needed or produced. Write a few language items of general interest on the board at the end.

Tip
> Leave students to think of their own examples for the final box in the framework. If they have problems, possible examples might include: a 'suggestions box', competitions like 'Employee of the month', a company newsletter, sports activities, recreational outings etc.

3 Discuss.

1 Which classroom management options will you follow? See pages 4–5.
2 Circulate during the discussion. Make a note of good/bad language use.

Feedback slot

See page 5.

Extension

- Students can write a short report on motivation through communication, involvement and recognition in their own companies.
- Consider repeating the activity in a later lesson e.g. with a different partner. See page 5.

31 Motivation through job satisfaction

1 Read the text and check the vocabulary.

Motivation does not just come from pay and promotion, although those are certainly important. Motivation also comes from feeling valued in your work and satisfied inside yourself. All managers have to give some attention to these non-material aspects of motivation, but Human Resources managers often have a key role. They can be divided into three related areas:

Communication

Do staff feel that lines of communication are good? How could they be improved? Are staff given regular feedback on how they are doing? How is this done? Is there an appraisal process? How does the process work?

Involvement

Involvement is the feeling that you are part of the company and not just working as an individual. For staff to feel fully involved they have to be given regular and meaningful opportunities to achieve, for example doing challenging tasks and taking part in interesting projects. Involvement often depends on how employees are consulted, and about which issues. Consultation can go further and become delegation. How do you decide which decisions and responsibilities are appropriate for each level in the company? How is this done without creating risks to the company?

Recognition

This is the public, official attention and thanks staff get for their actions and suggestions.

Conclusion

If the company culture gives a lot of attention to the above areas, then staff are likely to be committed in their work and loyal to the company. If not, then problems will appear such as low morale, high levels of sickness and time off work, high staff turnover, and high levels of grievances.

2 Write notes about your company.

Communication problems	Possible solutions
•	⟹
•	⟹

Case study: involvement through opportunities to achieve	
Case	Evaluation of case

Case study: involvement through consultation/delegation	
Case	Evaluation of case

Recognition, and other ways we build motivation, commitment and loyalty

3 Discuss.

Paul Emmerson © Cambridge University Press 2002 **Photocopiable**

HUMAN RESOURCES

32 Recruitment and selection

Before you start

1 Are your students interested in this topic? Use the checklist on page 7.
2 Which classroom management options will you follow? See pages 4–5.
3 Do your students need language support for the discussions? See page 8.

1 Prepare.

Task 1

1 Get students to read through the stages and check the vocabulary. (See *Vocabulary box* below.)

Vocabulary box

using an Executive Search agency: using a specialized, external organization to find a manager with the right skills and experience to do a particular job, often by persuading a suitable person to leave their present job

job description: an official list of the work and responsibilities involved in one particular job/position, also known as a *job specification*

advertise internally or externally: whether people from outside the company have a chance to apply

to apply for: to officially ask to be considered for a job, place on a course etc. by writing a letter

application form: a printed piece of paper on which you write the answers to questions

selecting: carefully choosing a particular person for a particular job. This word is more specific than *recruiting* which means generally finding new people to work in an organization.

CV: curriculum vitae – a document that lists your education and work experience; (US = *résumé*)

2 Get students to put the stages into a likely sequence. Elicit possible answers. (See *Possible answer* box opposite.)

Possible answer

Note that the sequence can vary and some early stages are mutually exclusive e.g. using an Executive Search and advertising. Likely sequence: c, d, a, f, b, e, i, h, j, g.

Task 2

Get students to decide if the words and phrases in each set are the same or different. (See *Answers* box below.)

Answers

1 These are synonyms in the context of recruitment.
2 *an applicant:* someone who asks to be considered for a job by completing an application form/sending a CV; *a candidate:* an applicant who has been called for an interview
3 These are synonyms in the context of recruitment.
4 These are opposites – *equal opportunities:* making sure that the same chances are given to everyone whatever their age, sex, race, religion etc.; *discrimination:* treating one person or group worse than others

5 *to recruit/to take on:* to find new people to work for an organization; *to hire* is very similar, but can refer to a person or organization and suggests that they are employed for a short time only.
6 *to dismiss/to fire:* to order an employee to leave their job, but *to fire* is more informal; *to make redundant/ to lay off:* these have nearly the same meaning, but here it is not the person's fault that they lose their job (perhaps it is due to economic circumstances). *To lay off* is more common in American English.

2 Write notes about the recruitment and selection process in your company.

1 Focus attention on the ideas maps and the grid and check the vocabulary in the headings.
2 Circulate while students make notes. Write down on a piece of paper any useful language needed or produced. Write a few language items of general interest on the board at the end.

3 Discuss.

1 Which classroom management options will you follow? See pages 4–5.
2 Circulate during the discussion. Make a note of good/bad language use.

Feedback slot

See page 5.

Extension

- Students can write a short report on recruitment and selection issues in their own companies.
- Consider repeating the activity in a later lesson e.g. with a different partner. See page 5.

32 Recruitment and selection

1 Prepare.

1 Put the following stages into a likely sequence.

 a deciding whether to use an Executive Search agency
 b choosing which publications and other media to advertise in
 c drawing up a job description
 d deciding whether to advertise internally or externally
 e interested people apply for the job and receive an application form
 f deciding on the content of the job advert
 g selecting one candidate and offering them the job
 h deciding on who to invite for an interview, then interviewing them
 i looking through all the completed application forms and CVs that you receive
 j drawing up a shortlist of candidates for a second interview

2 Same or different?

1 *a job, a position, a post*	4 *equal opportunities, discrimination*
2 *an applicant, a candidate*	5 *to recruit, to take on, to hire*
3 *headhunting, executive search*	6 *to dismiss, to fire, to make redundant, to lay off*

2 Write notes about the recruitment and selection process in your company.

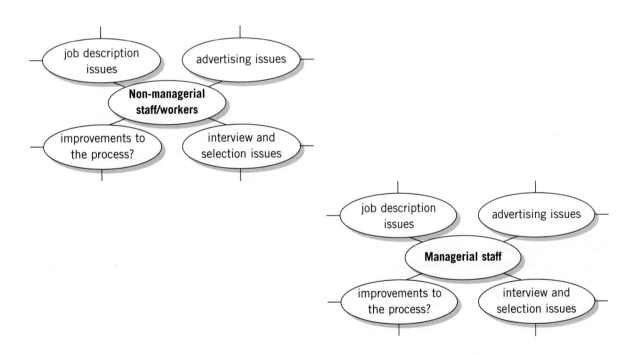

Case study: one recruitment and selection process	
Case	Evaluation of case

3 Discuss.

33 Training and team-building

Before you start

1 Are your students interested in this topic? Use the checklist on page 7.
2 Which classroom management options will you follow? See pages 4–5.
3 Do your students need language support for the discussions? See page 8.

1 Brainstorm.

1 Focus attention on the ideas maps and check the vocabulary in the headings. (See *Vocabulary box* below.)

Tip

Elicit the word for what you get when you train – *a skill*: a practical ability that you can learn, such as computing skills or communication skills.

Vocabulary box

off-the-job training: this means you go away from your workplace to do the training
training courses/programmes: these are synonyms
on-the-job training: this means you train while you are still actually doing your job (the training is *in-house* if it is provided by your own employees)
induction: showing a new recruit how to do their job and how the company runs
coaching: building people's skills and confidence in order to improve their performance and motivation. Coaching tends to have a specific goal, and is a term that comes from sport.
mentoring: helping someone to learn within the context of a supportive relationship. It is similar to coaching, but is only one-to-one and can involve wider, 'softer' issues such as support, advice etc. and tends not to have a specific goal.

apprentice: a young person who is being trained to do a skilled job, usually a manual job in a factory; an *apprenticeship* is the period of time when someone is an apprentice
secondment: a period of time you spend away from your usual job, usually doing another job in another office of the same company
job rotation: having an opportunity to do different jobs e.g. on a team or in different departments; *job swapping* would be exchanging jobs with one other person
sponsored MBAs: when a company pays all or part of the costs of a Master of Business Administration (MBA) degree
integration: when all the team members with their different skills and responsibilities work together well
conflict: serious disagreement
performance: how successful the team is, how well it works

2 Get students to brainstorm vocabulary in pairs or small groups.
3 Elicit answers and write them on the board. (See *Possible answers/ideas* box below.)

Tip

You can also get students to brainstorm verbs that collocate with *training course*:
to attend / complete / do / enrol on / follow / hold / organize / provide / run / start / take a training course.

Possible answers/ideas

Off-the-job training issues: evaluation (how do you know if it was successful?)
On-the-job training issues: evaluation (how do you know if it was successful?)
Career development issues: postings abroad (a period of

time when an employee is sent to another country to do a particular job)
Team-building issues: how the team is formed, team roles (e.g. leader, innovator, doer, analyst, supporter), activities like residential courses, measuring success

2 Write notes about training and team-building in your company.

1 Focus attention on the grids and check the vocabulary in the headings. Point out there is space in each grid to describe and evaluate some real-life cases.
2 Circulate while students make notes. Write down on a piece of paper any useful language needed or produced. Write a few language items of general interest on the board at the end.

3 Discuss.

1 Which classroom management options will you follow? See pages 4–5.
2 Circulate during the discussion. Make a note of good/bad language use.

Feedback slot

See page 5.

Extension

- Students can write a short report on training and team-building issues in their company.
- Consider repeating the activity in a later lesson e.g. with a different partner. See page 5.

33 Training and team-building

1 Brainstorm.

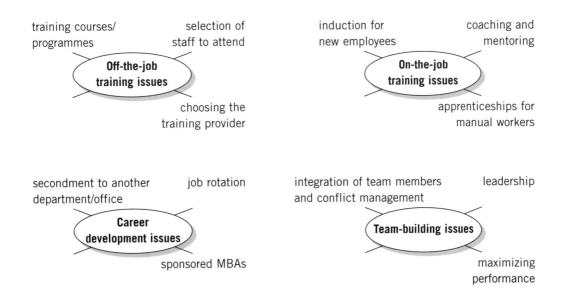

2 Write notes about training and team-building in your company.

Training: non-managerial staff/workers	
Off-the-job training issues	On-the-job training issues
Case study ⇨	Evaluation of case

Training: managerial staff	
Off-the-job training issues	On-the-job training issues
Case study ⇨	Evaluation of case

Team-building	
Case study ⇨	Evaluation of case

Other career development issues

3 Discuss.

34 Industrial relations

Before you start

1 Are your students interested in this topic? Use the checklist on page 7.
2 Which classroom management options will you follow? See pages 4–5.
3 Do your students need language support for the discussions? See page 8.

1 Read the text and check the vocabulary. Can you add anything?

Get students to read the text and underline any words they don't recognize. (See *Vocabulary box* below.)

Tip

The text is quite comprehensive, but students at a higher level in the company who are directly involved in industrial relations might be able to think of some points to add.

Vocabulary box

workforce: all the people who work in a company; a synonym for *employees* or *staff*

the availability of workers: the issue here is that if skilled workers are in short supply, the company will have to pay more to attract them

productivity: the rate at which goods are produced, and the amount produced, in relation to the work/time/money needed to produce them

industrial action: this can also include a *work-to-rule* (following every single rule in order to slow down work), a *go-slow* (when the workers deliberately work slowly), an *overtime* ban (refusing to work more than the normal hours) or a *boycott* (refusal to handle certain goods)

terms of employment: a written statement giving details of the employee's responsibilities, working hours, rate of pay etc.

sick pay: the money you are paid when you miss work because you are ill

maternity leave: the time you are allowed to be absent from your work because of being pregnant

grievance procedure: a *grievance* is something you complain about officially because you think it is unfair, so the *grievance procedure* is the steps that an employee should follow to resolve the problem e.g. first speak directly to their line manager, then if the grievance cannot be resolved, ask a union representative to take up the case etc.

redundancy arrangements: any compensation that might be paid to an employee because they have lost their job and it is not their fault e.g. layoffs due to the economic situation

dismissal: losing your job because you have not obeyed the rules. (Note the difference between *unfair dismissal* and *constructive dismissal* – the first is when someone is unfairly removed from their job by their employer, the second is when someone chooses to leave but feels they have been forced to leave e.g. their employer has treated them badly.)

disciplinary action: punishment

employment tribunal: a court that is given authority to deal with matters of employment law

safety: being safe from danger or bodily harm

working environment: a synonym for *workplace/place of work*

hazard: something that is dangerous

Safety Officer: the safety representative

safety policy: a written statement about safety that usually has to be on display in the workplace

safety procedures: the correct way to behave to stay safe

safety equipment: special equipment to prevent harm e.g. a wrist rest for someone who suffers from RSI (repetitive strain injury) or a metal guard to prevent parts of the body coming too close to dangerous equipment

protective clothing: clothes that protect the body e.g. a mask for the eyes or special headwear like a helmet on a civil construction site

2 Write notes on industrial relations issues in your company.

1 Focus attention on the grids and check the vocabulary in the headings. Tell students that they can describe and evaluate a real-life example in each area (a mini case study).
2 Circulate while students make notes. Write down on a piece of paper any useful language needed or produced. Write a few language items of general interest on the board at the end.

3 Discuss.

1 Which classroom management options will you follow? See pages 4–5.
2 Circulate during the discussion. Make a note of good/bad language use.

Feedback slot

See page 5.

Extension

- Students can write a short report on industrial relations in their company.
- Consider repeating the activity in a later lesson e.g. with a different partner. See page 5.

34 Industrial relations

1 Read the text and check the vocabulary. Can you add anything?

Industrial relations is the interaction between management and the workforce, with the workforce usually being organized into one or more trade unions. Human Resources managers are usually directly involved in industrial relations, and have to become specialized in matters of employment law, health and safety etc. Industrial relations covers a range of areas:

Pay bargaining

This is an annual process of negotiations, with any pay increase usually being related to the rise in the cost of living, the availability of workers, increases in other industries, recent increases in productivity etc. Workers may take industrial action e.g. go on strike, if they are not satisfied with the increase the company is offering. To resolve a dispute there may be an outside agency who can try conciliation (helping the two sides to reach an agreement) or arbitration (a process in law where a third party decides the outcome, which is usually a compromise between the two positions).

Employment contracts

Every employee has a contract that states their terms of employment. Areas covered typically include a job description, salary, pension scheme, hours of work, holiday leave, sick pay, maternity leave, grievance procedures, disciplinary rules, rights to belong to or not belong to a trade union, redundancy arrangements etc.

Dismissal procedures and employment protection

If a worker behaves badly or is bad at their job, it might be necessary to take disciplinary action against them, after a series of warnings. In extreme cases the employee might be dismissed. If the employee thinks this is unfair, they can appeal to an employment tribunal.

Health and safety

Employees need a safe working environment free of health hazards and accident risks, and this is often the responsibility of the Human Resources department. Often one member of staff is the Safety Officer (usually appointed by the union), and they have to check on the implementation of the safety policy and safety procedures (such as fire drills or the correct handling of dangerous materials). Employees may need safety equipment or protective clothing.

2 Write notes on industrial relations issues in your company.

Pay bargaining

Employment contracts

Dismissal procedures and employment protection

Health and safety

3 Discuss.

35 Trade and government policy

Before you start

1 Are your students interested in this topic? Use the checklist on page 7.
2 Which classroom management options will you follow? See pages 4–5.
3 Do your students need language support for the discussions? See page 8.

1 Prepare.

Task 1

Get students to check the vocabulary. (See *Vocabulary box* below.)

Tip

As a follow-up to this task, ask students which policies promote free trade and which ones limit it (with some policies the answer may be 'it depends').

Vocabulary box

assistance for exporters: this includes advice, trade delegations etc.
policy: strategy
balance of payments: the difference between the amount of money coming into a country and the amount going out
currency and capital flow restrictions: limits on the amount of money that can be moved into and out of the country e.g. repatriation of profits by multinationals
depreciation: loss of value
dumping: selling products cheaply in an export market, perhaps to increase market share and put other companies out of business
exchange rate: the value of a currency in comparison with another
incentive: something that encourages you to act in a particular way
interest rate: this is not directly under government control if there is an independent Central Bank (CB), but government policies will influence the CB's decisions

licensing: these include oil exploration, telecommunications bandwidth, TV channels
protectionism: the system of helping your country's trade, especially by taxing foreign goods
regional trading blocks: these include European Union (EU), North Atlantic Free Trade Association (NAFTA), Association of South East Asian Nations (ASEAN)
requirements for local sourcing/local managers/ technology transfer: when foreign manufacturers can set up a factory if they use local suppliers/managers and transfer high technology from their own countries
subsidy: money given by government to support an industry e.g. a strategic industry like agriculture
tariffs: taxes on goods coming into a country
quotas: limits on the amount of goods entering a country
tax policy: this includes company and individual direct and indirect taxes

Task 2

1 Focus attention on the table and check the vocabulary. (See *Vocabulary box* below.)

Tip

If students disagree on the classification of some items as positive or negative, use this to start a short discussion.

Vocabulary box

flexible: the opposite of *rigid/restrictive*
income: how much people earn; a synonym of *salary*
loyalty: a feeling of support
high skill levels: this means workers are well educated and able to do complex jobs
shareholder pressure: shareholders forcing the company to focus only on short-term profit

to use capital efficiently: to improve productivity, to increase efficiency, to cut costs, to invest profitably
the welfare state: government protection/social benefits for people who are poor, ill, not working etc.
trade union: an organization representing people working in a particular industry or profession that protects their rights

2 Get the students to discuss the questions in pairs or small groups. Then hold a short feedback session.

2 Write notes.

1 Focus attention on the grid and check the vocabulary in the headings.
2 Circulate while students make notes. Write down on a piece of paper any useful language needed or produced. Write a few language items of general interest on the board at the end.

3 Discuss.

1 Which classroom management options will you follow? See pages 4–5.
2 Circulate during the discussion. Make a note of good/bad language use.

Feedback slot

See page 5.

Extension

• Consider repeating the activity in a later lesson e.g. with a different partner. See page 5.

35 Trade and government policy

1 Prepare.

1 Look at the list of government policies. Check the vocabulary.

assistance for exporters   balance of payments policy   breaking up monopolies   control of public spending   currency and capital flow restrictions   depreciation of the currency   dumping   encouraging competition   exchange rate policy   incentives for inward investment   free trade   interest rate policy   liberalization   licensing   open borders   protectionism   privatization   regional trading blocks   regulation (and deregulation)   requirements for local sourcing/local managers/technology transfer   subsidies   tariffs and quotas   tax policy

2 Study the table below showing four economic 'models'. Then answer the questions.

	positive points	negative points
American model	flexible labour and product markets; low taxes; strong competition; shareholder capitalism puts pressure on managers to increase profits	wide income differences between rich and poor; poor quality of publicly-funded services like education and health; low investment; low savings rates
Japanese model	employees have loyalty to company; high skill levels; high quality public services; managers can take a long-term view because of absence of shareholder pressure	firms are protected from the full force of the market and have little pressure to use capital efficiently
East Asian model	low taxation; flexible labour markets; high levels of personal savings; open trade	sometimes a high level of government intervention in business
German/Scandinavian model	good education and training; a generous welfare state; social harmony because of narrow income difference between rich and poor; high investment from banks	taxes too high; some social benefits too high; trade unions too powerful; labour market and product market restrictions

- Do you think the four 'models' are more or less true? If not, what important points do they miss?
- Which 'model' is your country closest to? How is your country different? How is it changing?

2 Write notes.

The impact of ...	... on my market	... on my company
my own government's policies		
the policies of governments in countries I export to		
the policies of governments in countries I import from		

3 Discuss.

INTERNATIONAL TRADE

36 Exporting

1 Look at the ideas map. Which items are relevant to you?

Focus attention on the ideas map. Lead a discussion by asking students about the different items e.g. *What do you export? Why?* etc. (See the *Possible questions* box below for more ideas.)

Tip

Keep this stage quite brief. Remember that students will have a chance to prepare notes in the framework for a more detailed discussion.

Possible questions

Local agent issues

commission: How is it assessed?

targets: How are they set?

marketing support: What do you provide? e.g. sales literature, point-of-sale materials, anything else?

defining responsibilities: Is it clear what you do and what your local agent does? Who is responsible for promotion? What level of after-sales support will you provide? How much control do you expect over the way your product is sold?

additional point: Do you involve your foreign distributor in making your future development plans?

Marketing issues

promotion: What kinds? e.g. TV, newspapers, magazines, cinema, radio, street posters, others? How do you decide which means of promotion are appropriate? e.g. monitoring of competitors' advertising, cultural or geographical factors, timing according to when retail/industrial buyers place their orders, trade fairs,

local consumer preferences as to price against quality against guarantees, local legislation such as data protection laws affecting mailing lists, laws restricting advertising to children or laws related to products like alcohol or cigarettes

distribution: How do you control foreign distribution channels?

Other issues

transport: Do you use a freight forwarding company? Any problems with this?

problems with official documents: see Teacher's notes for framework 37

Additional points

domestic government assistance with exporting; foreign government controls and regulations; political risks; exchange rate risks; different language and legal processes; different accounting/tax systems; different technical standards established in law

2 Write notes about your own company.

1 Focus attention on the grids and check the vocabulary in the headings.
2 Circulate while students make notes. Write down on a piece of paper any useful language needed or produced. Write a few language items of general interest on the board at the end.

3 Discuss.

1 Which classroom management options will you follow? See pages 4–5.
2 Circulate during the discussion. Make a note of good/bad language use.

Feedback slot

See page 5.

Extension

• Students can write a short summary of their company's present and future export strategy.
• Consider repeating the activity in a later lesson e.g. with a different partner. See page 5.

36 Exporting

1 Look at the ideas map. Which items are relevant to you?

2 Write notes about your own company.

What?	Where to?
Why?	How much?

How? (e.g. own sales organization or agent?)

	Typical problems	Typical solutions
Local agent issues	•	⇨
	•	⇨
Marketing issues	•	⇨
	•	⇨
Other issues	•	⇨
	•	⇨

Future export strategy

3 Discuss.

37 Importing

1 Look at the ideas map. Which items are relevant to you?

Focus attention on the ideas map. Lead a discussion by asking students about the different items e.g. *What do you import? Why?* etc. (See the *Possible questions* box below for more ideas. The box contains a list of the well-known 'INCOTERMS' for reference. Ask students to explain only the ones that they use and do not mention the others. Have a Business English dictionary available in the classroom.)

Tips

- Keep this stage quite brief. Remember that students will have a chance to prepare notes in the framework for a more detailed discussion.
- A useful verb for discussions about importing is *to source:* to obtain materials and parts from all over the world, usually for reasons of cost. A common collocation is *global sourcing.*

Possible questions

General issues

intermediary: e.g. wholesaler, agent, or distributor?
additional points: risk management i.e. What would you do if there was a serious problem with your overseas supplier? Have you ever had problems with government controls such as arranging an import licence?

Local production issues

quality and technical issues: e.g. difficulty in dealing with problems when Head Office in your country is a long way from the production site

Payment issues

exchange rate fluctuations: How do you minimize the losses produced by movements between currencies?
terms of payment: these include INCOTERMS – the part of the contract that states the exact point where the supplier's obligations for transport and insurance costs end and the buyer's begin. The most common are Cost and Freight (CFR), Cost, Insurance and Freight (CIF), Carriage and Insurance Paid to (CIP), Carriage Paid to (CPT), Delivered

at Frontier (DAF), Delivered Duty Paid (DDP), Delivered Duty Unpaid (DDU), Delivered ex Ship (DES), Delivered ex Quay (DEQ), Free Alongside Ship (FAS), Free Carrier (FCA), Free on Aircraft (FOA), Free on Board (FOB)

Transport and logistics issues

transport arrangements: air, sea, road, rail, and then main advantages and disadvantages of each
official documents: these can be divided into five types:
1 commercial documents e.g. invoice, pro-forma invoice
2 official documents e.g. certificate of health, certificate of origin, export licence, the Single Administrative Document within the European Union
3 transport documents e.g. airway bill, shipping note, maritime bill of landing
4 insurance documents e.g. certificate of insurance, insurance policy
5 financial documents related to payment e.g. letter of credit, open account, advance payment, support by a bank guarantee

2 Write notes about your own company.

1 Focus attention on the grids and check the vocabulary in the headings.
2 Circulate while students make notes. Write down on a piece of paper any useful language needed or produced. Write a few language items of general interest on the board at the end.

3 Discuss.

1 Which classroom management options will you follow? See pages 4–5.
2 Circulate during the discussion. Make a note of good/bad language use.

Feedback slot

See page 5.

Extension

- Students can write a short summary of their company's present and future import strategy.
- Consider repeating the activity in a later lesson e.g. with a different partner. See page 5.

37 Importing

1 Look at the ideas map. Which items are relevant to you?

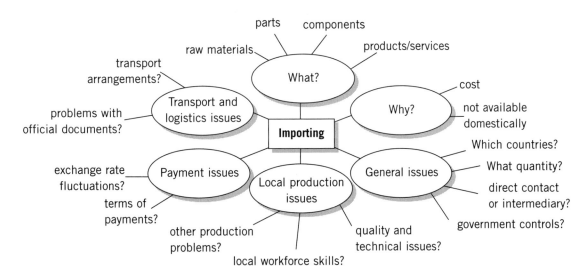

2 Write notes about your company.

What?	Where to?
Why?	How much?

How? (e.g. direct contact with foreign supplier or agent?)

	Typical problems	Typical solutions
Local production issues	•	⇨
	•	⇨
Payment issues	•	⇨
	•	⇨
Transport and logistics issues	•	⇨
	•	⇨
Other issues	•	⇨
	•	⇨

Future plans

3 Discuss.

38 Manufacturing location

Before you start

1 Are your students interested in this topic? Use the checklist on page 7.
2 Which classroom management options will you follow? See pages 4–5.
3 Do your students need language support for the discussions? See page 8.

Tip

This framework assumes that students were or will be involved in a decision about manufacturing location.

1 Prepare.

Task 1

1 Focus attention on the ideas maps and check the vocabulary in the headings. (See *Vocabulary box* below.)
2 Get students to brainstorm further ideas in pairs or small groups.

Tip

Point out that there are spaces on the ideas map for students to brainstorm a few more ideas.

Vocabulary box

National issues

trade barriers: taxes (*tariffs*) or restrictions on volume (*quotas*) that make trade between two countries more difficult and therefore cause a company to close down its factories in one place and reopen somewhere else
currency fluctuations: movements in the exchange rate
Additional point: language

Site issues

regional incentives: money or special tax arrangements given by local or national government to help develop a particular area
Additional point: room for further expansion

Financing issues

access to grants and loans: money given by government (a *grant*) or lent by a bank (a *loan*)
Quality of life issues
housing/shops/schools/cultural facilities: these are necessary to attract and retain managers

Task 2

Get the students to discuss the questions below the ideas maps in pairs or small groups. Then hold a short feedback session.

Tip

Keep this stage quite brief. Remember that students will have a chance to prepare notes in the framework for a more detailed discussion.

2 Write notes about your company's manufacturing location.

1 Focus attention on the ideas map and check the vocabulary in the headings.
2 Circulate while students make notes. Write down on a piece of paper any useful language needed or produced. Write a few language items of general interest on the board at the end.

3 Discuss.

1 Which classroom management options will you follow? See pages 4–5.
2 Circulate during the discussion. Make a note of good/bad language use.

Feedback slot

See page 5.

Extension

- Students can write a short report on their reasons for choosing the particular location they discussed, or analysing options if they are in the process of making a decision about the future.
- Consider repeating the activity in a later lesson e.g. with a different partner. See page 5.

38 Manufacturing location

1 Prepare.

1 Check the vocabulary. Then brainstorm more ideas for deciding on a manufacturing location.

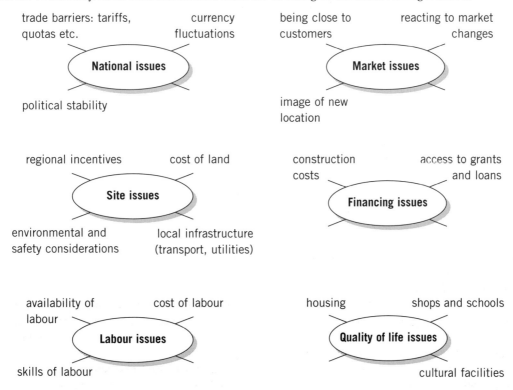

trade barriers: tariffs, quotas etc.   currency fluctuations   **National issues**   political stability

being close to customers   reacting to market changes   **Market issues**   image of new location

regional incentives   cost of land   **Site issues**   environmental and safety considerations   local infrastructure (transport, utilities)

construction costs   access to grants and loans   **Financing issues**

availability of labour   cost of labour   **Labour issues**   skills of labour

housing   shops and schools   **Quality of life issues**   cultural facilities

2 Are/Were you involved in a real-life decision about manufacturing location? What are/were the alternative sites you are considering/considered?

2 Write notes about your company's manufacturing location.

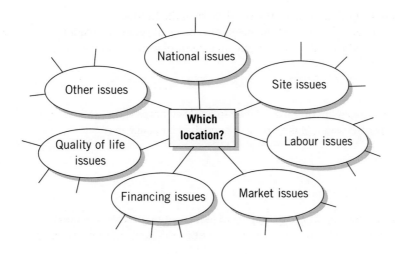

National issues · Other issues · Site issues · Quality of life issues · Which location? · Labour issues · Financing issues · Market issues

3 Discuss.

Teacher's notes Economic and social context: 39 Globalization

39 Globalization

Before you start

1 Are your students interested in this topic? Use the checklist on page 7.
2 Which classroom management options will you follow? See pages 4–5.
3 Do your students need language support for the discussions? See page 8.

1 Brainstorm.

1 Focus attention on the ideas maps and check the vocabulary in the headings. (See *Vocabulary box* below.)

Vocabulary box

wages: a close synonym of *salaries*, but *wages* is used more often for workers in a factory and *salaries* for managers and professionals. The word *wages* is nearly always used in discussions about globalization, low pay etc.
sourcing: obtaining parts and materials from a particular place; *logistics:* distributing the finished goods to the customer. So *global sourcing and logistics* refers to the fact that parts and materials can be obtained from anywhere in the world rather than traditional domestic suppliers, and that there are global solutions for distribution such as parcel services, shipping, air freight etc.

2 Get students to brainstorm further vocabulary and ideas in pairs or small groups.
3 Elicit answers and write them on the board. (See *Possible answers/ideas* box below.)

Possible answers/ideas

Advantages: increases competition between companies; makes clean/green technologies available to everyone; increases job opportunities for people in poorer countries
Disadvantages: increases environmental damage in poor countries; destroys local industries; gives too much power to multinational companies
Market forces driving globalization: a saturated home market; customers expecting a global presence; reduced product development times; the development of regional trading blocks (See framework 35.)

Cost factors driving globalization: government assistance – both help with exporting from the home government and support for inward investment from the foreign government
Technology driving globalization: computer networks; video conferencing; management information tools such as expert systems, customer relations management software, intranets and extranets etc.

2 Write notes.

Tasks 1 and 2

1 Focus attention on the grids and check the vocabulary in the headings.
2 Circulate while students make notes. Write down on a piece of paper any useful language needed or produced. Write a few language items of general interest on the board at the end.

3 Discuss.

1 Which classroom management options will you follow? See pages 4–5.
2 Circulate during the discussion. Make a note of good/bad language use.

Feedback slot

See page 5.

Extension

• Students can write a short report on the impact of globalization on their business.
• Consider repeating the activity in a later lesson e.g. with a different partner. See page 5.

39 Globalization

1 Brainstorm.

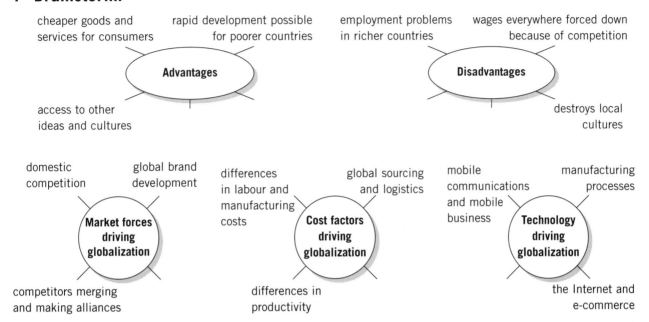

cheaper goods and services for consumers

rapid development possible for poorer countries

Advantages

access to other ideas and cultures

employment problems in richer countries

wages everywhere forced down because of competition

Disadvantages

destroys local cultures

domestic competition

global brand development

Market forces driving globalization

competitors merging and making alliances

differences in labour and manufacturing costs

global sourcing and logistics

Cost factors driving globalization

differences in productivity

mobile communications and mobile business

manufacturing processes

Technology driving globalization

the Internet and e-commerce

2 Write notes.

1 How is globalization affecting your business?

Market forces driving globalization	
Evidence in my market	Impact on my company

Cost factors driving globalization	
Evidence in my market	Impact on my company

Technology driving globalization	
Evidence in my market	Impact on my company

2 What is your personal view of globalization? List two good things and two bad things.

1 _____   1 _____

2 _____   2 _____

3 Discuss.

40 Social responsibility

Before you start

1 Are your students interested in this topic? Use the checklist on page 7.
2 Which classroom management options will you follow? See pages 4–5.
3 Do your students need language support for the discussions? See page 8.

1 Tick the boxes to show the priorities in your company.

1 Get students to read the questionnaire and underline any words they don't recognize.
(See *Vocabulary box* below.)

Vocabulary box

harm: trouble or damage caused by someone's actions
toxic: poisonous
pollution: damage caused to the environment by harmful chemicals and waste
recycled: put through a process so that it can be used again
to minimize: to make something that is not wanted as small as possible

waste: materials which are left after you have used something and which you want to get rid of
enviromentally-friendly: not damaging the environment
packaging: the bags, boxes etc. in which goods are sold
charity: an organization with a legal status that gives help to people who need it

2 Get students to complete the questionnaire individually by ticking the relevant boxes.

2 Write notes.

1 Focus attention on the grids and check the vocabulary in the headings.
2 Circulate while students make notes. Write down on a piece of paper any useful language needed or produced. Write a few language items of general interest on the board at the end.

Tips

- Explain that a *social/environmental audit* is a detailed assessment of the impact of the company on the communities where it operates and on the natural environment. Audits of this kind are increasingly common, particularly in Europe where there is pressure for them to be done every year alongside the financial audit.
- The final box could include, for example, 'green marketing' where companies refer to issues such as the recyclable nature of their products as a marketing tool.

3 Discuss.

1 Which classroom management options will you follow? See pages 4–5.
2 Circulate during the discussion. Make a note of good/bad language use.

Feedback slot

See page 5.

Extension

- Students can write a short summary of their company's social responsibility policies, or that of their partner.
- Consider repeating the activity in a later lesson e.g. with a different partner. See page 5.

40 Social responsibility

1 Tick the boxes to show the priorities in your company.

	High priority	Medium priority	Low priority	Not relevant
Preventing or reducing harm				
keeping a safe workplace and reducing accidents	○	○	○	○
reducing noise, smells, toxic chemicals and other pollution inside the factory	○	○	○	○
reducing noise, smells, toxic chemicals and other pollution outside the factory	○	○	○	○
Conserving and protecting resources				
using recycled materials in the production process	○	○	○	○
minimizing solid and liquid wastes	○	○	○	○
reusing waste products from the production process	○	○	○	○
use of environmentally-friendly packaging	○	○	○	○
Responsibility to the local community				
providing childcare and health-care for workers	○	○	○	○
providing sports and leisure facilities for workers	○	○	○	○
supporting local education and arts projects	○	○	○	○
giving money to charities and other non-profit organizations	○	○	○	○
supporting positive social change e.g. by recruitment policies	○	○	○	○
consulting local people and local government about plans	○	○	○	○

2 Write notes.

Choose three high/medium priority areas from those above and give details.

1

2

3

Are there any other ways that your company reduces health risks, protects the environment or contributes to the community?

Has your company ever had to do an official social or environmental audit? Give details.

How do you integrate social and environmental issues with your business and marketing plans?

3 Discuss.

ECONOMIC AND SOCIAL CONTEXT

41 The changing workforce

Before you start

1 Are your students interested in this topic? Use the checklist on page 7.
2 Which classroom management options will you follow? See pages 4–5.
3 Do your students need language support for the discussions? See page 8.

1 Read these statements and check the vocabulary.

1 Get students to read the statements and underline any words they don't recognize. (See *Vocabulary box* below.)

Tips

- The statements are, of course, deliberately controversial. Tell students that they will have a chance to discuss them all at the end, after they have prepared their ideas.
- Another useful word in this context is *discrimination*: when one group of people is treated differently and unfairly by another.

Vocabulary box

networking: meeting other people who do the same type of work in order to share information and help each other
consensus: general agreement between everyone in a group
rewards: these include money, company cars, praise, status etc. for doing good work
to retain: to keep

2 Write notes.

Tasks 1 and 2

1 Focus attention on the grid and check the vocabulary in the question in task 2.
2 Circulate while students make notes. Write down on a piece of paper any useful language needed or produced. Write a few language items of general interest on the board at the end.

3 Discuss.

1 Which classroom management options will you follow? See pages 4–5.
2 Circulate during the discussion. Make a note of good/bad language use.

Feedback slot

See page 5.

Extension

- Students can write a short summary of how their own company's workforce is changing.
- Consider repeating the activity in a later lesson e.g. with a different partner. See page 5.

41 The changing workforce

1 Read these statements and check the vocabulary.

1 Women often receive less pay than men for doing the same job.
2 Women managers often hit a 'glass ceiling' – an invisible barrier on the career ladder beyond which they cannot pass.
3 There is a 'feminine management style'. It has more emphasis on communication, networking, collecting ideas from others, cooperation and participation, building consensus, sharing power and information, good interpersonal relationships.

   There is also a 'masculine management style'. It has more emphasis on rewards, clearly defined tasks, command and control structures.
4 Successful organizations in the future will need to find a balance between the two styles, with the feminine style being more valued than it is now.
5 Older employees are not valued by organizations. They are always looking over their shoulder at younger people trying to take their jobs for less money. It's difficult for them to find a new job if they want to. If a company is in trouble, they are forced to take early retirement.
6 Successful organizations in the future will need to do more to retain older, experienced employees.

2 Write notes.

1 Do you agree with statements 1–6 above? What is the situation in your company? Write notes on each statement.

	My opinions	Situation in my company
1		
2		
3		
4		
5		
6		

2 A diverse workforce is made up of men and women, young and old, different races and religions, disabled and able-bodied, different lifestyles etc. What are the special problems in managing a diverse workforce?

_____

_____

_____

_____

3 Discuss.

42 The future of work

1 Prepare.

1 Get students to read the text and underline any words they don't recognize. (See *Vocabulary box* below.) Then get students to discuss the points in pairs or small groups.

Tip

The statements are, of course, deliberately controversial to encourage discussion. Students may express different views from those in the text.

Vocabulary box

trends: tendencies in the way a situation is changing
rates: speeds (in this context)
freelancing: when a professional person works independently for several different organizations
to be self-employed: having your own business rather than being employed by a company
hire and fire: a fixed expression that means 'recruit and dismiss'
marketable skills: practical abilities to do a job that companies want
overwork: too much work

social benefits: these includes sick pay, holiday pay, pension plans etc.
pension: the money you receive when you retire, either from the government (the state pension) or from a private pension company
core group: a central group
to network: to meet other people who do the same type of work in order to share information and help each other etc.

2 Students brainstorm other ways in which work is changing. There is no suggested answer here, as this depends on individual situations and opinions.

Tip

If your group has not done framework 41, you could feed in some of the ideas in the statements on page 91.

2 Write notes.

Tasks 1 and 2

1 Focus attention on the grid in task 1 and the ideas map in task 2. Check the vocabulary in the headings.
2 Circulate while students make notes. Write down on a piece of paper any useful language needed or produced. Write a few language items of general interest on the board at the end.

3 Discuss.

1 Which classroom management options will you follow? See pages 4–5.
2 Circulate during the discussion. Make a note of good/bad language use.

Feedback slot

See page 5.

Extension

- Students can write a short summary of the future of work in their profession.
- Consider repeating the activity in a later lesson e.g. with a different partner. See page 5.

42 The future of work

1 Prepare.

1 Read the text and check the vocabulary. Do you agree with all the points?

The following trends seem to be developing, although at different rates in different countries:

– people are changing jobs more frequently.
– there is more use of temporary contracts and freelancing.
– there is more working from home.
– more people want to be self-employed.
– it is easier to hire and fire workers.

Some negative aspects include:

– the difficulty of career planning.
– the increasing inequality between those with marketable skills and those without.
– overwork and long hours caused by insecurity; people having less time with their families.

In general, there is more opportunity, but also more uncertainty. So:

– **governments** have to make labour markets more flexible, support training, extend social benefits to people without permanent contracts, and make saving for a pension more flexible.
– **companies** need to think about how to manage and integrate temporary staff, how to keep a core group of workers who can maintain the company culture.
– **individuals** have to keep learning new skills, look for opportunities to network with useful future contacts, think of themselves as a 'brand' that needs building and marketing.

2 How else is work changing?

2 Write notes.

1 Which trends are happening in your profession? Choose three and write notes.

Trend		How I notice it day-to-day
1	⇨	
2	⇨	
3	⇨	

2 How is your government responding? And your company? And what about you?

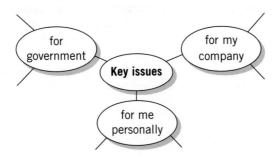

3 Discuss.

INFORMATION TECHNOLOGY

43 IT management

Before you start

1 Are your students interested in this topic? Use the checklist on page 7.
2 Which classroom management options will you follow? See pages 4–5.
3 Do your students need language support for the discussions? See page 8.

Tip
This framework does not deal with the whole area of e-commerce and the Internet. This is covered in framework 44 where it can be discussed in more detail.

Tip
Check comprehension of *IT*. It stands for *Information Technology* and it includes both computer technology and communications technology.

1 What do IT managers have to think about? Brainstorm.

1 Focus attention on the ideas maps and check the vocabulary. (See *Vocabulary box* below.)

Vocabulary box

system: here this means a client/server system. The server is the main piece of hardware that runs and controls all the individual client PCs on people's desks (these are joined together in a network).

hardware: computer equipment, rather than programs

hacker: someone who tries to get into another person's computer system in order to see, use, change or damage the information

firewall: a system that stops people looking at certain information on a computer, especially to protect company information from hackers and viruses

systems software: this includes, for example, Windows, Unix, Linux, Oracle, utilities etc.

applications software: this includes, for example, word processors, databases, spreadsheets etc.

to liaise: to exchange information so that everyone knows what is happening

integration: checking that all the software works together

legacy systems: old hardware/software that is still used

cost-benefit analysis: a way of calculating methods or plans to bring you the most benefits for the smallest cost

device: a piece of equipment

mobile devices: these include any piece of communications equipment that can be carried easily such as a mobile phone, PDA (personal digital assistant) or a combination of the two

video conferencing: allowing virtual meetings where participants from anywhere in the world can appear on the same screen together and see and talk to each other

intranet: a closed, private part of the Internet that is used for exchanging information within a company; an *extranet* is like an intranet, but there is selected access to the system to people from outside the company e.g. customers and suppliers.

2 Get students to brainstorm further vocabulary and ideas in pairs or small groups.
3 Elicit answers and write them on the board. (See *Possible answers/ideas* box below.)

Possible answers/ideas

Systems administration: No suggestions given here as it depends on individual situations.
Purchasing new hardware/software: Upgrade path (future possibilities to improve the system); future-proofing (making sure that your system can be used in the future); real cost of ownership (i.e. all the hidden costs like the cost to the company when the system is not working etc.)
Other issues: No suggestions given here as it depends on individual situations.

2 Write notes.

Tasks 1 and 2

1 Focus attention on the grids and check the vocabulary in the headings and in the questions. (See *Vocabulary box* opposite.)

Vocabulary box

customization: designing and building a product especially for one customer, but the customized product is often based on a standard product
off-the-shelf: standard
tailor-made: customized

2 Circulate while students make notes. Write down on a piece of paper any useful language needed or produced. Write a few language items of general interest on the board at the end.

3 Discuss.

1 Which classroom management options will you follow? See pages 4–5.
2 Circulate during the discussion. Make a note of good/bad language use.

Feedback slot

See page 5.

Extension

• Students can write a short report on IT management in their own company.

43 IT management

1 What do IT managers have to think about? Brainstorm.

systems software problems

hardware problems

applications software problems

systems security: passwords,
hackers, viruses, firewalls

Systems administration

liaising with outside
consultants

cost-benefit analysis
for new hardware

cost-benefit analysis for
new software

Purchasing new hardware/software

integration of new
hardware/software
with legacy systems

liaising with
outside consultants

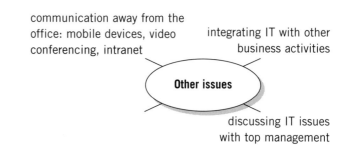

communication away from the
office: mobile devices, video
conferencing, intranet

integrating IT with other
business activities

Other issues

discussing IT issues
with top management

2 Write notes.

1 What are the current issues and future opportunities and challenges in IT management
in your company?

Systems administration	
Current issues	Future opportunities and challenges
•	•
•	•

Purchasing new hardware/software	
Current issues	Future opportunities and challenges
•	•
•	•

Other issues

2 Customization is a big issue for IT managers:
- Off-the-shelf package or tailor-made solution? How do you decide?
- What degree of customization? How do you decide?
- How do you customize?

3 Discuss.

Teacher's notes Information technology: 44 E-commerce

44 E-commerce

Tip

> This framework relates to frameworks 43 and 45, so your students may want to work on them as a set.

1 Check the vocabulary and concepts. Can you add anything?

Get students to read the three lists and underline any words/concepts they don't understand. (See *Vocabulary box* below.)

Vocabulary box

e-commerce: electronic commerce – buying and selling goods and services over the Internet

cost reduction: cutting down printing and postage costs by having information on-line; automating processes that were previously done by people, such as data entry, answers to FAQs (frequently asked questions) etc.

speed: speed of finding out information, speed of ordering, speed of contacting company by e-mail etc.

personalization: automatic log-in; ease of finding specific information through menus and search engines; ease of putting together a personalized order; automatic re-entry of delivery or payment instructions etc.

global reach: customers can access site from anywhere in the world; 24-hour presence; smaller product niches can become profitable; dispersed communities of customers can become closer to each other and to your organization

measurement: the *log file* on the *host computer* holds information about how visitors used the site that can then be used in management decisions

fulfilment: delivering the right goods to the customer at the promised time

site map: the structure of the website in terms of which pages lead to which other pages, often shown as a tree-diagram

links: the words you can click on to take you to other websites

monitoring traffic: checking how many people came to the site (*the hits*), who they were, where they came from, the route they took, how long they spent, the products they looked at, the products they bought

security: this includes making sure that *the server* (the main computer) is secure i.e. safe from hackers, viruses etc. and also *encryption* (turning information into a special code so that only certain people can use it e.g. credit card information is encrypted when it is sent over the Internet)

promoting an on-line presence: putting the web address or URL (Unique Resource Locator) on company material like letterheads, advertisements, posters etc.; on-site promotions such as special offers, competitions etc.; *spamming* (sending out e-mail advertisements that the computer user has not asked for)

banner ads and pop-up windows: these are adverts for your company on another website

2 Write notes.

Tasks 1 and 2

1 Focus attention on the grids and ideas map and check the vocabulary in the headings.
2 Circulate while students make notes. Write down on a piece of paper any useful language needed or produced. Write a few language items of general interest on the board at the end.

3 Discuss.

1 Which classroom management options will you follow? See pages 4–5.
2 Circulate during the discussion. Make a note of good/bad language use.

Feedback slot

See page 5.

Extension

- Students can write a short summary of e-commerce in their own company.
- Consider repeating the activity in a later lesson e.g. with a different partner. See page 5.

44 E-commerce

1 Check the vocabulary and concepts. Can you add anything?

The benefits of e-commerce
1 cost reduction
2 speed
3 personalization
4 global reach
5 measurement

Impact of e-commerce on general business activity
1 impact on products: price and product range
2 impact on costs (particularly IT costs)
3 impact on order processing, stock management and fulfilment
4 impact on customer service and after-sales
5 impact of e-commerce systems on other IT systems

Issues in website management
1 Front-end/design issues: site map, choice of text and graphics, links, ease of navigation, ease of ordering
2 Back-end/technical issues: content management system for updating and managing data on the site, monitoring traffic on the site, security
3 Promoting an on-line presence: promoting the web address, registration with search engines and directories, banner ads and pop-up windows on other sites, on-site promotions, e-mail promotions

2 Write notes.

1 Write about e-commerce in your market/company.

Background: history of e-commerce in my market/company

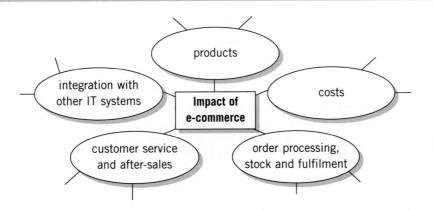

Future of e-commerce in my market/company

2 Are you involved in website management? What issues are important at the moment?

3 Discuss.

45 Using business software

Before you start

1 Are your students interested in this topic? Use the checklist on page 7.
2 Which classroom management options will you follow? See pages 4–5.
3 Do your students need language support for the discussions? See page 8.

Tip

This framework relates to frameworks 43 and 44, so your students may want to work on them as a set.

1 Read the text and check the vocabulary.

Get students to read the text and underline any words they don't recognize. (The different types of software are explained in the text but see the *Vocabulary box* below for other vocabulary.)

Tip

Encourage students to think of other types of software not included in the text, or other important trends in software.

Vocabulary box

payroll: a list of all the people employed by a company, and the records of how much money they have been paid

to track: to follow the progress of something

call centre: an office where people answer questions, make sales etc. over the telephone; (US = *customer service center*)

inventory: stock

procurement: the act of finding, ordering and buying equipment and supplies

2 Write notes about your own company.

1 Focus attention on the grid and check the vocabulary in the headings.
2 Circulate while students make notes. Write down on a piece of paper any useful language needed or produced. Write a few language items of general interest on the board at the end.

3 Discuss.

1 Which classroom management options will you follow? See pages 4–5.
2 Circulate during the discussion. Make a note of good/bad language use.

Feedback slot

See page 5.

Extension

- Students can write a short report on past and present uses of software in their company.
- Consider repeating the activity in a later lesson e.g. with a different partner. See page 5.

45 Using business software

1 Read the text and check the vocabulary.

In the early days of computers, business software was dominated by office applications, in particular word processing, spreadsheets, databases, presentations software and accounting software. In addition, there was specialist software in areas like computer-aided design and manufacture. The next phase, during the 1990s, saw large companies starting to use software packages for areas like corporate finance and financial planning, stock control and some human resources functions such as payroll.

Now companies need to invest in other types of software. E-business software is needed to run a website and take orders. Customer relationship management systems help companies to track their sales activities, make customer service more efficient, and plan marketing campaigns. Sales staff use it to get customer information over the Internet, and it can also be used to improve automation of call centres. Supply chain software tracks the inventory that a company holds, allows real-time communication between the company and its suppliers, and then automates the process of ordering parts. Collaborative software allows co-workers inside a company to share information via the Internet and work on documents and projects together in real time from different locations. It can also be used to work with counterparts from other companies, for example engineers can talk together about plans and product design. And e-learning is an area that could become very important in the future.

There are also many entirely Web-based services. For example, procurement services allow companies to find the cheapest price or the fastest delivery time for a whole range of supplies, and logistics services allow shippers and transport companies to bid for jobs and so develop the most efficient delivery plan possible. Also, there is an increasing trend for much of the software mentioned in the previous paragraphs to move away from company's own computers and onto the Internet.

Things change quickly in the software industry, but one thing always remains the same. You have to pay big consultants' fees to make it all work.

2 Write notes about your own company.

	last few years	next few years
changes in my business due to developments in software		
changes in my own job due to developments in software		
procedures for evaluating and purchasing new software		
training, maintenance and dealing with problems		

3 Discuss.

CULTURAL AWARENESS

46 Cultural values at work

Before you start

1 Are your students interested in this topic? Use the checklist on page 7.
2 Which classroom management options will you follow? See pages 4–5.
3 Do your students need language support for the discussions? See page 8.

Tip

In this framework students compare their own country with another country. Get students to look at the options in section 1 carefully. If students choose an interview, it could be in class with a classmate or outside the class with a colleague/friend. If it is outside the class, it could be in person or by telephone. Another option is that students could choose the United States as the 'other country', and fill in that column based on their knowledge from films, TV programmes etc.

1 Prepare.

Tasks 1, 2 and 3

1 Get students to read the instructions and check the vocabulary in the table. (See *Vocabulary box* below.)

Vocabulary box

care and formality: this could include holding the card with two hands, studying it, asking questions, putting it on table during the meeting, putting it away carefully in a special case etc.

gestures: movements of the head or hand

physical contact: this includes arm holding, back slapping etc.

hierarchy: a system in which people are arranged into levels according to their importance

Tips

There are other cross-cultural issues not included in the table for reasons of space. You could also mention the following points if students are interested:

• Meetings – How important is punctuality? How much small talk is there before getting down to business? Is respect shown for age and company position in a meeting e.g. seating, who speaks first and last? How acceptable is humour in a business meeting? How acceptable is smoking in a meeting? How important is making and circulating a written record of the meeting (*the minutes*)?
• Gifts – What value? What kind? To an individual or the group?

2 Get students to choose who to interview. If the interviews happen in class e.g. pairs interviewing each other about countries they have worked in, allow plenty of time for this. Finish all the interviews before moving on to individual note-writing in section 2.

Tip

If students fill in the table in section 1 based on their own experience, then the framework in section 2 is a follow-up stage. If students do an interview in section 1, then they will complete section 2 separately, reflecting on the interview. The personal story will be one of their own.

2 Write notes.

1 Focus attention on the grids and check the vocabulary in the headings.
2 Circulate while students make notes. Write down on a piece of paper any useful language needed or produced. Write a few language items of general interest on the board at the end.

3 Discuss.

1 Which classroom management options will you follow? See pages 4–5.
2 Circulate during the discussion. Make a note of good/bad language use.

Feedback slot

See page 5.

Extension

• A discussion topic to extend the activity would be 'How much of our behaviour is due to individual personality, and how much to culture?' Another topic could be 'When doing business in other countries, should you try to behave like the locals, or should you be yourself. How do you get the right balance between the two?'
• Students can write a short report on cultural differences at work, or a summary of what they found out from the interview.
• Consider repeating the activity in a later lesson e.g. with a classmate from (or with experience of) another country. See page 5.

46 Cultural values at work

1 Prepare.

1 You are going to compare your country with another country. You can use your own experience, or interview someone who knows about business culture in another country.

The interview could be with:
- a colleague/friend/classmate who has worked in another country.
- a colleague/friend/classmate who comes from another country.

2 Study the list of habits and customs in the table below.

3 Use your experience, or do the interview, to compare the two countries. Complete the empty boxes by writing a number from 1 to 5:

1 for habits and customs that are uncommon or unimportant
5 for habits and customs that are very common or very important

	My country	Other country		My country	Other country
1 Business cards are exchanged with care and formality on first meeting.			11 Top managers take most decisions – there isn't much consultation.		
2 Titles like Doctor, Engineer are used to show educational background.			12 Important decisions are taken outside meetings.		
3 Colleagues move quickly to first names after a few meetings.			13 The English language is used in most meetings in large companies.		
4 Colleagues shake hands every morning in the office.			14 People interrupt and disagree freely in meetings.		
5 People communicate in an expressive way with gestures and physical contact.			15 Teamwork and cooperation are highly valued.		
6 People kiss women colleagues on the cheek.			16 Presentations are formal, with little audience interaction until the end.		
7 Most business people, and all managers, wear formal, well-made clothes.			17 People discuss business at lunch.		
8 Time is spent building a personal relationship before doing business.			18 People socialize with clients outside work e.g. golf, going to bars.		
9 Business culture is based on goals, results and short-term profit.			19 People give gifts to clients.		
10 Hierarchies are flat, with small status and salary differences between levels.			20 Women are treated as equals in business, in practice not just in theory.		

2 Write notes.

Find the biggest differences

A personal story about a cross-cultural misunderstanding

Background:

What happened:

Reason for misunderstanding:

Consequences:

3 Discuss.

47 Cultural values in society

Before you start

1 Are your students interested in this topic? Use the checklist on page 7.
2 Which classroom management options will you follow? See pages 4–5.
3 Do your students need language support for the discussions? See page 8.

Tips

- See the Teacher's notes for framework 46. The option of choosing the United States as the 'other country' and drawing on films, TV programmes etc. is also possible in this framework.
- This framework is more abstract than framework 46, and is likely to appeal to more intellectual students or those with a higher educational level.

1 Prepare.

Tasks 1, 2 and 3

1 Get students to read the instructions and check the vocabulary in the table. (See *Vocabulary box* below.)

Vocabulary box

cultural values: ideas about what is important in life, principles, ways of thinking

destiny: things that will happen in the future

fatalistic: believing that people cannot change events

objectivity: not being influenced by your own feelings and opinions

subjectivity: being influenced by your own feelings and opinions

competitive: when people try to be more successful than others

individualistic: doing things your own way, without being influenced by other people

achievement: succeeding in doing something difficult through your own efforts

cooperative: willing to help

collectivist: when things are shared or done by all members of the group together

loyalty: being faithful to something, supporting something

analytical: using a logical method to think about something, especially by looking at all the parts separately

holistic: examining the whole of something, not just parts of it

2 Get students to choose who to interview. If the interviews happen in class e.g. pairs interviewing each other about countries they have worked in, allow plenty of time for this. Finish all the interviews before moving on to individual note-writing in section 2.

2 Write notes.

1 Focus attention on the grids and check the vocabulary in the headings.
2 Circulate while students make notes. Write down on a piece of paper any useful language needed or produced. Write a few language items of general interest on the board at the end.

Tip

If students fill in the table in section 1 based on their own experience, then the framework in section 2 is a follow-up stage. If students do an interview in section 1, then they will complete section 2 separately, reflecting on the interview. The personal story will be one of their own.

3 Discuss.

1 Which classroom management options will you follow? See pages 4–5.
2 Circulate during the discussion. Make a note of good/bad language use.

Feedback slot

See page 5.

Extension

- A further discussion topic might be 'How can we use this information when doing business in other cultures?'
- Students can write a short report on cultural differences in society, or a summary of what they found out from the interview.
- Consider repeating the activity in a later lesson e.g. with a classmate from (or with experience of) another country. See page 5.

47 Cultural values in society

1 Prepare.

1 You are going to compare your country with another country. You can use your own experience, or interview someone who knows about the culture of another country.

The interview could be with:
- a colleague/friend/classmate who has worked in another country.
- a colleague/friend/classmate who comes from another country.

2 Study the list of values and ways of thinking below.

3 Use your experience, or do the interview, to compare the two countries.
Write the first letter of the country in the appropriate place on the scales below.

Control over events
People believe they make their own destiny and can control events.

|----|----|----|----|----|----|----|----|

People are fatalistic and believe events are controlled by chance or luck.

Approach to tasks and time
People work one task at a time with a single focus. Tasks are completed punctually by following plans.

|----|----|----|----|----|----|----|----|

People work on many tasks at the same time. Tasks have flexible completion times.

Communication: directness
Communication is direct. Information exchange is simple, clear and verbal. Indirectness is frustrating and suspicious.

|----|----|----|----|----|----|----|----|

Communication is indirect. A lot of information is unspoken but clear from the situation. Directness is seen as aggressive.

Communication: relationships
Communication is impersonal. Facts and figures are important. A high degree of objectivity.

|----|----|----|----|----|----|----|----|

Communication is personal. Relationships are important. An emphasis on subjectivity.

Structure and conflict
People are comfortable with flexible structures and unpredictable situations. Disagreement with authority is acceptable.

|----|----|----|----|----|----|----|----|

There is a high need for order and rules. Conflict is threatening. Disagreement with authority is rare.

Individualism and competition
The culture is competitive and individualistic. Independence is valued. Achievement and material success are important.

|----|----|----|----|----|----|----|----|

The culture is cooperative and collectivist. Loyalty to the group is valued. The quality of life and relationships are important.

Thinking style
Thinking style is analytical. Problems are broken down and each piece is treated separately.

|----|----|----|----|----|----|----|----|

Thinking style is holistic. A focus on the whole picture and the way the parts are related.

2 Write notes.

Key differences between the two countries	Values becoming similar due to globalization
	Values resisting change

Differences in cultural values: a personal story

3 Discuss.

Paul Emmerson © Cambridge University Press 2002 **Photocopiable**

48 Working in another culture

Before you start

1 Are your students interested in this topic? Use the checklist on page 7.
2 Which classroom management options will you follow? See pages 4–5.
3 Do your students need language support for the discussions? See page 8.

Tip

If students chose to do interviews in frameworks 46 and 47, then this framework would make a good follow-up in a later lesson.

1 Prepare.

Tasks 1 and 2

1 Get students to read the instructions and check the vocabulary in the lists. (See *Vocabulary box* below.)

Tip

This framework deliberately makes no distinction between national culture and company culture in order to make the range of questions and answers as open as possible. You may want to mention this distinction at the end as an extension to the discussion in section 3.

Vocabulary box

trends: tendencies, developments

taboo: something you should not talk about because people think it is morally wrong or embarrassing; *taboo topics* that typically show a cultural difference are talking about salary and talking about sensitive political questions. Some topics like religion are taboo for socializing in nearly all cultures.

2 Get students to write their questions.

2 Interview the person and make notes on the answers.

1 Students carry out the interview and make notes on the answers in the right-hand column.
2 If the interview is in class, circulate while students make notes. Write down on a piece of paper any useful language needed or produced. Write a few language items of general interest on the board at the end.

3 Discuss your answers. Compare your own country.

1 Which classroom management options will you follow? See pages 4–5.
2 Circulate during the discussion. Make a note of good/bad language use.

Feedback slot

See page 5.

Extension

- Students can write a short summary of what they found out from the interview.
- Consider repeating the activity in a later lesson e.g. with a classmate from (or with experience of) another country. See page 5.

48 Working in another culture

1 Prepare.

1 You are going to interview a business person from another country or someone from your own country who has worked abroad. You could:
- interview a colleague/friend/classmate.
- interview the person face to face or by telephone.

2 Study the list of possible questions about business culture in another country. You might think of other questions not on the list. Then look at section 2 below and write ten questions you want to ask.

Economy: government policies about trade/privatization etc.? economic trends (inflation etc.)?
Company management style: focus on people or results? culture of leadership or delegation? focus on individual or team? formal or informal company culture? flat or hierarchical organization structure?
Working life: times of the working day/week? holidays? is changing jobs/cities common?
Meetings: decision-making or information sharing? strong chairperson? clear roles?
Presentations: formal or informal? interaction with the audience? questions at the end?
Negotiations: fast or slow? direct or indirect style? need to refer to boss for final decision? tactics?
Socializing: safe topics and taboo topics? gifts when you are invited to someone's house? who pays in the bar/restaurant? what kind of humour is common?

2 Interview the person and make notes on the answers.

Questions	Answers (notes)
1	
2	
3	
4	
5	
6	
7	
8	
9	
10	

3 Discuss your answers. Compare your own country.

49 Discussing news items

Before you start

1 Are your students interested in this topic? Use the checklist on page 7.
2 Which classroom management options will you follow? See pages 4–5.
3 Do your students need language support for the discussions? See page 8.

Tips

- You may need to bring some newspapers and magazines into class to distribute round the group, although students also have the option of just choosing a story they know about (with no text). Weekend business supplements are particularly good as they tend to analyse rather than just report the story. Alternatively, students can find the texts at home.
- If you are going to let students choose articles from magazines that you bring in, they don't have to choose in class. You can give a whole magazine to each student and ask them to choose an article at home.
- Point out that students can use an article in their own language as a source of ideas. This has an advantage in that students have to focus on the meaning and can't copy parts of the original.
- At the time of writing, *The Economist* and *Financial Times* both offer a free weekly e-mail news service. Subscription is very easy. You can simply print out the text for use in class.

1 Prepare.

Establish that students are going to choose and then summarize two news items for group discussion. They may know some stories without any further input needed by the teacher (things they would talk about normally in their own language), or they may need some texts to give them ideas. (See *Tips* box above.)

Tips

- Encourage different students to use different news stories.
- The texts don't have to be long articles – one-line summaries of the type you get down the side of a newspaper front page or in an e-mail news service are fine.

2 Choose two items of recent business news and write notes.

1 Focus attention on the grids and check the vocabulary in the headings.
2 Circulate while students make notes. Write down on a piece of paper any useful language needed or produced. Write a few language items of general interest on the board at the end.

3 Discuss.

1 Which classroom management options will you follow? See pages 4–5.
2 Circulate during the discussion. Make a note of good/bad language use.

Feedback slot

See page 5.

Extension

- Students can write a short summary of their news items, or those of their partner.
- Consider repeating the activity in a later lesson e.g. with a different partner. See page 5.

49 Discussing news items

1 Prepare.

Here are some places where you can find business news:
- your own knowledge of what has been happening in the business world
- articles in English-language newspapers and magazines
- articles published in your country in your language
- by e-mail by registering at the websites of well-known newspapers and magazines (usually free)

2 Choose two items of recent business news and write notes.

News item 1	
What happened?	Implications for the future
Background information	My own opinions
Why I chose this story	Questions to other people to find out their opinions

News item 2	
What happened?	Implications for the future
Background information	My own opinions
Why I chose this story	Questions to other people to find out their opinions

3 Discuss.

50a Using an authentic text

Tips
- This framework will involve students working with longer texts and giving a more structured summary, unlike framework 49 which is suitable for use with no text or with short texts.
- You can bring some newspapers and magazines into class. Weekend business supplements are particularly good. Students can choose an article in class, or take a newspaper/magazine and choose at home.
- Alternatively, students can find texts at home.

1 Prepare.
Task 1
1 This task encourages students to think about their vocabulary development strategies when using authentic texts. Get students to briefly discuss the missing type of vocabulary in b. Elicit answers from the students. (See *Answer* box opposite.)
2 Get students to discuss the advantage of focusing on words in group b. Elicit answers from the students. (See *Possible answers/ideas* box below.)

Answer
Type b is: *words I know but don't use.*

Possible answers/ideas
Words in group b are part of the students' passive vocabulary. Focusing on the words will help to activate them, and this is useful and achievable on a short course.

Some of the words in group c may be important to learn, but many will be difficult, low frequency, journalistic, or with cultural references that a student cannot understand. Students need to learn to select useful vocabulary.

Task 2
Hand out an article to each student or let them choose their own.

Tasks 3–6
Get students to read the instructions and check the vocabulary.

Tip
Point out that task 5 specifies *words and phrases* rather than just *words* and introduce or remind students about word partnerships (collocations) and semi-fixed and fixed expressions. Encourage students to record these and put them onto the ideas map as well as single words.

2 Make an ideas map.
1 Get students to complete the ideas map, for homework or in class.
2 If in class, circulate while students make notes. Write down on a piece of paper any useful language needed or produced. Write a few language items of general interest on the board at the end.

3 Discuss, now or in the next class.
Tasks 1 and 2
1 Which classroom management options will you follow? See pages 4–5. Get students to read the instructions and check the vocabulary.
2 Circulate during the discussion. Make a note of good/bad language use.

Feedback slot
See page 5.

Extension
Students can try to reconstruct the article using just the ideas map.

Tips
- Pointing to the words as they are spoken gives a strong visual/kinesthetic reinforcement.
- Task 2 can be done immediately, or in another lesson. It is a useful aid to fluency and vocabulary acquisition.

50a Using an authentic text

1 Prepare.

1 When you read an authentic text there are three types of vocabulary. What is type b?

  a words I know and can use

  b

  c words I don't know

  What is the advantage of focusing on words in group b?

2 Choose an article, or look at the article the teacher gives you.

For homework or in class

3 Read the text once or twice for general understanding.

4 Make an ideas map of the main points in the article. Use the diagram in section 2 and:

  • put one word or a single phrase in the middle box to summarize the article.
  • decide what are the main points in the article (probably there will be three or four) and write them as short phrases in ovals 1, 2, 3 and 4.
  • look again at the individual points, opinions, facts and figures in the article and write them in your own words at the end of the lines on the ideas map.

5 On a separate piece of paper make a list of words and phrases from the article that are in group b (vocabulary that you know but don't use actively). Choose the vocabulary carefully – words and phrases that you often need.

6 Now try to include the words and phrases from your list on the ideas map in an appropriate place. You may need to extend the map with a few more lines.

2 Make an ideas map.

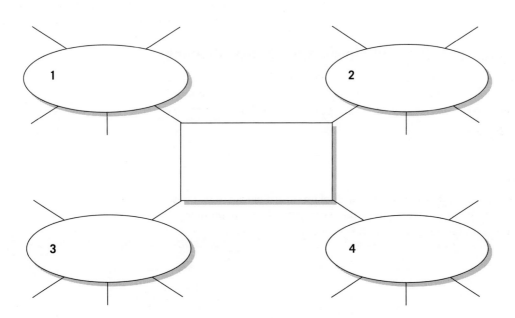

3 Discuss, now or in the next class.

1 Explain your diagram to a partner. Use a pen to point to words and ideas as you mention them.

2 Work with a new partner. Turn over your sheet and explain the article again.

50b Using an authentic text

(based on an original idea by Mark Powell)

Before you start

1 Are your students interested in this topic? Use the checklist on page 7.
2 Which classroom management options will you follow? See pages 4–5.
3 Do your students need language support for the discussions? See page 8.

Tips

- This framework will involve students working with longer texts and giving a more structured summary, unlike framework 49 which is suitable for use with no text or with short texts.
- You may need to bring some newspapers and magazines into class to distribute round the group. Weekend business supplements are particularly good as they tend to analyse rather than just report the story. Alternatively, students can find the texts at home.
- If you are going to let students choose articles from magazines that you bring in, they don't have to choose in class. You can give a whole magazine to each student and ask them to choose an article at home.

1 Prepare for homework.

Tasks 1–3

Get students to read the instructions and check the vocabulary. Point out that task 2 has some phrases to use in the text summary and task 3 encourages students to think about their vocabulary development strategies when using authentic texts.

2 Write your summary.

Get students to write their summary.

Tips

- The framework assumes the students will do the writing at home. They can do it in class, but it may take up a lot of classtime.
- If students need more space, they can continue on the back of the sheet.

3 Read your summary out slowly and clearly. Discuss.

1 Which classroom management options will you follow? See pages 4–5.
2 Get students to read out their summary and then discuss the content.
3 Circulate during the discussion. Make a note of good/bad language use.

Feedback slot

See page 5.

Extension

Students can turn over their sheets and explain the article again to a new partner without looking. This can be done straightaway, or in another lesson. It is a useful aid to fluency and vocabulary acquisition.

50b Using an authentic text

1 Prepare for homework.

1 Choose a news article that interests you, in English or your own language. Choose something that will interest the other students as well.

2 Study these sentence beginnings. You will use some in section 2 to write a summary of the article in English.

I was reading this article the other day in … and it talks about …
I chose this article because …
First of all, the article discusses the question of … It says that … According to …
Next, it talks about … It says that …
What's the explanation for this? Well, the article suggests that …
The article finishes by discussing … It says that …
What really interested me about the article was …
What surprised me was …
So how will all this affect us? Well, it seems that … However, … Basically, it all depends on …
Before I finish I'd like to mention one or two points of my own. I believe that … In addition, … Therefore, …
So, as we've seen, the article raises an interesting question, namely …
I'd like to begin the discussion by asking you what you think.

3 Read these tips for writing your summary.

- Use mainly your own words when you write. It will sound more natural when you read out your summary and you get more practice in English.
- Avoid trying to understand every word in the text. Many words will not be important to learn.
- Some words from the text will be useful to practise. In particular, look for words and phrases that you recognize and know are important but are unable to use actively when you speak. Practise these words by including them in the summary.

2 Write your summary.

_____

_____

_____

_____

_____

_____

_____

_____

_____

_____

_____

_____

(Continue on another page if necessary.)

3 Read out your summary slowly and clearly. Discuss.

Thanks and acknowledgements

Author's acknowledgements

I would like to thank Sally Searby at CUP for her expert guidance on this project and Will Capel for his initial interest. I'm also grateful to Amanda Maris for her careful editing and overall understanding of how the material should work.

Thanks also to John Nicholas for very useful comments on an early version of this book, and to colleagues at the International House Executive Centre, London, for comments on individual frameworks. In particular, thanks to Nick Hamilton, Charles Lowe, Susanna Damman and Belinda Cerda.

In addition, I would like to acknowledge the pioneering role played by Sharon Nolan and Bill Reed, who understood the particular nature of Business English long before the rest of us.

Publisher's acknowledgements

The author and publishers would like to thank the following for their help in reviewing and piloting the material and for the invaluable feedback which they provided: Rebecca Chapman, Business Language Center, Vienna; Jane Cordell, Ewan Jones, ACT Advanced Corporate Training, Warsaw; Anne Williams, Linguarama, UK; Bernie Hayden.